The History of The Ottoman Empire

CRAFTED BY SKRIUWER

Dear Reader,

Imagine crouching in the dust-choked foothills of Söğüt as Ertuğrul's warriors scan the horizon for Mongol raiders. Or standing breathless before Constantinople's walls in 1453, feeling the earth tremble under Ottoman cannons as centuries of Byzantine rule crumble. That's where this book begins: not with sterile dates, but with the sweat, ambition, and soul of an empire that reshaped continents.

As you turn these pages, you'll stand beside:

Frontier ghazis carving a beylik from Seljuk ruins, their loyalty forged around campfires in Anatolia's wilds (Chapters 1-2)

Mehmed the Conqueror, aged 21, watching his flagship breach the Golden Horn's chain — "The spider weaves curtains in the palace of Caesars" (Chapter 7)

Suleiman's architects sketching the Süleymaniye's domes while slaves haul marble under Istanbul's blistering sun (Chapter 11)

Janissary recruits trembling as the devşirme scribe inscribes their names — severing ties to family forever (Chapter 17)

We've woven this epic to reveal how Ottoman echoes shape our world:
- 🔥 *How 13th-century beylik alliances foreshadowed modern power blocs*
- 🔥 *Why Suleiman's legal codes still influence Balkan bureaucracies*
- 🔥 *How the empire's collapse ignited today's Middle Eastern borders*

This isn't just history — it's the blueprint of empires. When you witness:

Bayezid I's hubris before Timur's war elephants (Chapter 4), you'll see the peril of overextension

Köprülü viziers purging corruption (Chapter 14), you'll recognize desperate reform

Tanzimat reformers penning equality edicts (Chapter 16), you'll feel the tension between tradition and change

Pour strong Turkish coffee. Let's ride from the Anatolian steppes to Vienna's gates — through sieges, betrayals, and golden ages. May these stories not just inform you... but redefine how you see East and West.

With respect,
Skriuwer

Copyright © 2025 by Skriuwer.

All rights reserved. No part of this book may be used or reproduced in any form whatsoever without written permission except in the case of brief quotations in critical articles or reviews.

At **Skriuwer**, we're more than just a team—we're a global community of people who love books. In Frisian, "Skriuwer" means "writer," and that's at the heart of what we do: creating and sharing books with readers worldwide. Wherever you are in the world, **Skriuwer** is here to inspire learning.

Frisian is one of the oldest languages in Europe, closely related to English and Dutch, and is spoken by about **500,000 people** in the province of **Friesland** (Fryslân), located in the northern Netherlands. It's the second official language of the Netherlands, but like many minority languages, Frisian faces the challenge of survival in a modern, globalized world.

We're using the money we earn to promote the Frisian language.

For more information, contact : **kontakt@skriuwer.com** (www.skriuwer.com)

Historical Research Methodology

This work synthesizes information from:

- **Primary Sources**

    - Government archives and historical records
    - Period correspondence and eyewitness accounts
    - Contemporary newspapers and publications

Disclaimer:
The images in this book are creative reinterpretations of historical scenes. While every effort was made to accurately capture the essence of the periods depicted, some illustrations may include artistic embellishments or approximations. They are intended to evoke the atmosphere and spirit of the times rather than serve as precise historical records.

"History is the version of past events that people have decided to agree upon."

– Napoleon Bonaparte

THEY SAID IT: THE MOST EXPLOSIVE QUOTES

"We must do with the Greeks as we did with the Armenians."

– Talaat Bey (1917, Austro-Hungarian consular report 4).

"Kill every Greek they pass on the road."

– Rafet Bey (1916, Austro-Hungarian telegram 4).

"We will cut off your heads... Either we survive or you."

– General Mahmut Şevket Paşa (1909, to Greek Patriarch 4).

"At last we've uprooted the Greeks."

– Mustafa Kemal (1923, Turkish Grand National Assembly 49).

"Reduce Christian houses below Muslims'—or sell to us."

– Petition of al-Ḥājj Muṣṭafā (1742, Ottoman court document 11).

"Turkifying the nation demands exterminating all Christians."

– Henry Morgenthau Sr. (1915, diary quoting Talaat 410).

"This revolt ends 400 years of Ottoman tyranny!"

– Sharif Hussein ibn Ali (1916, Mecca proclamation 7).

"Sovereignty is seized by force—not Allah's gift."

– Namık Kemal (1870s, banned essay 2).

OTTOMAN EMPIRE HISTORY AT A GLANCE

A Visual Timeline of the History of the Ottoman Empire

● Pre-1299: Anatolian Foundations -

- Seljuk Sultanate of Rum fragments into rival beyliks (1077–1308),
- Mongol invasions devastate Anatolia (1243),
- Ertuğrul establishes Kayı tribe foothold at Söğüt (1230s),
- Turkic ghazi warrior culture merges with Sufi orders.

⛵ 1299–1453: Beylik to Empire -

- Osman I declares independence (1299),
- Orhan captures Bursa – first Ottoman capital (1326),
- Devşirme (child levy) system formalized (1360s),
- Bayezid I crushed by Timur at Ankara (1402),
- Mehmed II conquers Constantinople (1453).

🕌 1453–1566: Imperial Zenith -

- Suleiman's law code (Kanunname) centralizes power (1530–1540),
- Janissaries become dominant military force (1520s),
- Siege of Vienna repelled (1529),
- Ottoman fleet dominates Mediterranean (Barbarossa at Preveza, 1538).

⚔ 1566–1699: Stagnation & Revolts -

- Battle of Lepanto shatters naval supremacy (1571),
- Janissary corps corrupts (ocak devlet içinde devlet*, 1580s),
- Celali rebellions ravage Anatolia (1596–1610),
- Treaty of Karlowitz cedes Hungary to Habsburgs (1699).

📜 1700–1789: Reform Attempts -

- Tulip Era (Lâle Devri) cultural flowering (1718–1730),
- Patrona Halil rebellion ends Westernization push (1730),

- Köprülü viziers restore military discipline (1656–1702),
- First permanent Ottoman embassies in Europe (1720s).

🚂 1789–1839: Crisis & Adaptation -

- Selim III's Nizam-ı Cedid reforms crushed by Janissaries (1807),
- Greek War of Independence begins (1821),
- Mahmud II destroys Janissaries (Vaka-i Hayriye, 1826),
- Muhammad Ali of Egypt invades Syria (1831–1833).

💥 1839–1876: Tanzimat Reforms -

- Hatt-ı Şerif of Gülhane declares equality (1839),
- Crimean War exposes military weakness (1853–1856),
- First Ottoman constitution drafted (1876),
- Nationalist uprisings in Balkans (Serbia 1867, Bulgaria 1876).

⛏ 1876–1908: Autocracy & Resistance -

- Abdülhamid II suspends constitution (1878),
- Armenian massacres (1894–1896),
- Hijaz Railway project advances German influence (1900–1908),
- Young Turk Revolution forces restoration of parliament (1908).

🏴 1908–1922: Collapse & War -

- Balkan Wars erase European territories (1912–1913),
- Armenian Genocide (1915–1916),
- Arab Revolt with British support (1916–1918),
- Allied occupation of Istanbul (1918),
- Turkish War of Independence begins (1919).

🏛 1923–Present: Legacy & Successors -

- Republic of Turkey proclaimed (1923),
- Caliphate abolished (1924),
- Millet system's legacy fuels regional conflicts (e.g., Cyprus, Lebanon),
- Ottoman administrative traditions endure in Arab states (Jordan, Iraq).

TABLE OF CONTENTS

CHAPTER 1: THE EARLY TURKMEN BEGINNINGS (13TH CENTURY ORIGINS)

- *The decline of the Seljuk Sultanate of Rum and emergence of Turkish beyliks*
- *The Mongol invasions and their impact on Anatolia*
- *Ertuğrul and the establishment of the Ottoman foothold around Söğüt*
- *Frontier society, tribal dynamics, and early administrative practices*

CHAPTER 2: THE RISE OF OSMAN I AND ESTABLISHMENT OF THE OTTOMAN BEYLIK

- *Osman's early leadership and the Battle of Bapheus*
- *Key conquests against the Byzantine Empire*
- *Administrative seeds, alliances, and the role of Sufi orders*
- *The siege of Bursa and Osman's lasting legacy*

CHAPTER 3: EXPANSION UNDER ORHAN AND MURAD I

- *Consolidation of Bursa as the first Ottoman capital*
- *Introduction of the first Ottoman coins and further administrative steps*
- *Strategic marriages and diplomatic relations*
- *Murad I's push into the Balkans (notably in Thrace and beyond)*

CHAPTER 4: BAYEZID I AND THE TIMURID INVASION

- *The ambitious expansion campaigns of Bayezid I (Yıldırım)*
- *Internal consolidation: centralizing power over other beyliks*
- *Threats from European coalitions and battles in the Balkans*
- *The Battle of Ankara (1402) and the devastating Timur invasion*

CHAPTER 5: THE INTERREGNUM & THE RISE OF MEHMED I

- *Power vacuum following Bayezid I's capture*
- *Fierce rivalry among Bayezid's sons and the civil war*
- *Mehmed I's eventual triumph and reunification of Ottoman territories*
- *Reestablishing stability and trust among local populations*

CHAPTER 6: THE AGE OF MURAD II

- *Challenges to Ottoman authority from both East and West*
- *Murad II's battles in the Balkans and encounters with Crusader forces*
- *Diplomatic maneuvers and pacts with rival states*
- *Periods of abdication and return to power*

CHAPTER 7: THE CONQUEST OF CONSTANTINOPLE BY MEHMED II

- *Succession and vision of a young Mehmed II*
- *Siege warfare innovations and the fall of Constantinople (1453)*
- *Consequences for Eastern Christendom and global trade routes*
- *Transformation of the city into the Ottoman capital*

CHAPTER 8: MEHMED II'S REFORMS AND CONQUESTS AFTER 1453

- *Administrative and legal restructuring: Kanun and central bureaucracy*
- *Cultural patronage and architectural developments*
- *Further expansions in Eastern Europe, the Black Sea region, and Anatolia*
- *Integration of diverse populations under Ottoman rule*

CHAPTER 9: THE REIGN OF BAYEZID II & SHIFTS IN POWER

- Bayezid II's approach to governance and consolidation
- Diplomacy with emerging European powers
- Internal opposition and conflicts with Prince Cem
- Prelude to the empire's next major expansions

CHAPTER 10: SELIM I (SELIM THE GRIM) AND EASTERN EXPANSION

- Rise of Selim I and clashes with Safavid Persia
- Victories against the Mamluks and control of holy cities (Mecca, Medina)
- Reorganization of power in the Middle East
- Establishment of the Ottoman sultan as a leading figure in the Islamic world

CHAPTER 11: THE GOLDEN AGE UNDER SULEIMAN THE MAGNIFICENT

- Suleiman's legislative reforms and the epithet "the Lawgiver"
- Military campaigns in Hungary, Rhodes, and beyond
- Patronage of arts, architecture, and the imperial court
- Diplomatic relationships with European states

CHAPTER 12: LATER REIGNS OF THE 16TH CENTURY AND INTERNAL DEVELOPMENTS

- Succession struggles and court intrigues
- Shifts in the balance of power with Venice and Habsburg realms
- Economic challenges and changes in the global trade environment
- Continued architectural and cultural patronage

CHAPTER 13: DECLINE? REASSESSING THE 17TH CENTURY

- *Debates on the concept of "decline" versus transformation*
- *Military reforms and challenges on multiple fronts*
- *Rising tensions in the provinces and court factionalism*
- *Significant battles and treaties shaping Ottoman-European relations*

CHAPTER 14: KÖPRÜLÜ ERA AND ATTEMPTS AT REVIVAL

- *The Köprülü family of grand viziers and their strong leadership*
- *Efforts to restore military discipline and administrative efficiency*
- *Successes and failures in pushing back European advances*
- *Long-term implications of the Köprülü reforms*

CHAPTER 15: THE LONG 18TH CENTURY AND SHIFTING GLOBAL POWERS

- *Key treaties with European powers (e.g., Karlowitz, Passarowitz)*
- *Internal social dynamics, tax revolts, and local autonomy*
- *Rise of Russia as a major threat in the Black Sea region*
- *Cultural changes and Western influences at the Ottoman court*

CHAPTER 16: THE ERA OF REFORMS (TANZIMAT AND EARLY 19TH CENTURY)

- *Efforts to modernize the military, bureaucracy, and legal codes*
- *Edicts such as the Hatt-ı Şerif of Gülhane*
- *Growing tension between reformists and conservative factions*
- *European involvement in Ottoman internal affairs*

CHAPTER 17: MAHMUD II, ABDÜLMECID I, AND THE CHANGING FACE OF THE EMPIRE

- *Mahmud II's destruction of the Janissary Corps (the Auspicious Incident)*
- *Centralization efforts and administrative overhauls*
- *New educational institutions and Western-style governance*
- *Abdülmecid I's continuation of Tanzimat principles*

CHAPTER 18: CONTINUED REFORM EFFORTS AND INTERNAL STRUGGLES IN THE LATE 19TH CENTURY

- *Further constitutional attempts under Abdülhamid II*
- *Nationalist movements and the weakening of imperial cohesion*
- *Financial crises and European control over Ottoman debts*
- *Social and intellectual movements shaping the future of the empire*

CHAPTER 19: THE EARLY 20TH CENTURY, INTERNAL CHALLENGES, AND EXTERNAL PRESSURES

- *Discontent leading to the Young Turk Revolution*
- *Reforms, new constitutions, and the struggle for parliamentary governance*
- *Unrest in the Balkans and the ripple effects of nationalist uprisings*
- *Geopolitical rivalries with European powers*

CHAPTER 20: THE EMPIRE'S FINAL DECADES AND LEGACY

- *The empire's last efforts to maintain sovereignty*
- *Impact of wars and shifting alliances on Ottoman stability*
- *The cultural, social, and political heritage left behind*
- *Reflections on six centuries of Ottoman influence in the region and beyond*

CHAPTER 1

THE EARLY TURKMEN BEGINNINGS (13TH CENTURY ORIGINS)

The Ottoman Empire did not begin as a massive empire spanning three continents. Rather, it had its roots in the turbulent times following the Mongol invasions of the 13th century, when the once-mighty Seljuk Sultanate of Rum was fracturing into smaller Turkish principalities, or beyliks, across Anatolia. This period was marked by political fragmentation, shifting alliances, and competition for resources in the region. It was during this era that a small group of Turkmen, under a leader named Ertuğrul, would lay the groundwork for what would become the Ottoman state.

Turkmen Migrations and the Seljuk Background

To fully understand the origins of the Ottomans, one must go back to the broader history of the Turks in Anatolia. The Seljuk Turks began to enter Anatolia in significant numbers after the Battle of Manzikert in 1071, where they defeated the Byzantine army. Over time, the Seljuk Sultanate of Rum established itself across central Anatolia, blending Persian, Turkic, and local Byzantine influences.

However, by the early 13th century, the Sultanate of Rum was weakened by internal strife and by constant pressure from the Mongols. The Mongol invasions that swept across Asia eventually reached Anatolia, compelling smaller Turkish tribes and beyliks to move westward in search of safer territories. Many of these groups were warrior nomads, led by chieftains or beys who enjoyed a large degree of autonomy.

Among these migrating Turkmen was a leader named Ertuğrul, father of Osman I, who is considered the founder of the Ottoman state. Sources about Ertuğrul's life are limited and often shrouded in legend, but the broad strokes suggest he led his people from eastern or central parts of Anatolia toward the western frontiers of the collapsing Seljuk realm. Ertuğrul is said to have offered military assistance to a Seljuk sultan in a local conflict, receiving a small territory around Söğüt and Domaniç (in modern-day Turkey) as a reward. This region was strategically located on the frontier with the Byzantine Empire, which set the stage for future conquests.

Life on the Frontier

The frontier (or "uç" in Turkish) was an important concept. This zone between the shrinking Byzantine territories and the Turkish beyliks [principalities] was often controlled by frontier lords, known for their raiding and warrior culture. It was a harsh environment but also one of opportunity. These frontier warriors could gain territory, wealth, and followers through successful skirmishes against rival beyliks or Byzantine strongholds. Over time, the frontier beyliks gained renown for their martial prowess and accumulated both land and revenues.

The population in these border regions was mixed. There were local Christians (both Greek-speaking and Armenian communities), Turkish migrants, and even other groups like Orthodox monks living in monasteries. The frontier beys had to manage these diverse peoples, employing tolerant or pragmatic policies that allowed them to maintain stability and economic growth. Over time, these beyliks developed administrative systems, but they remained relatively loose compared to the highly centralized empires that the Ottomans would later build.

Early Administrative Practices

During these early decades, governance was fluid. Leadership was based largely on personal charisma and success in warfare. Ertuğrul, and later his son Osman, granted villages or pastoral lands to loyal followers in return for military service. Religious figures also played a key role in legitimizing the beys' authority. Sufi orders, in particular, became influential in spreading Islam and forging alliances.

The interplay between spiritual leaders and the political class would remain significant throughout Ottoman history.

While exact details are scarce, we can infer that these early Ottomans inherited practices from the Seljuks and other Turkmen principalities. This included certain administrative titles, the collection of tribute, and the tradition of assigning fiefs to warriors (timar system, which would become more formalized in the coming centuries).

At this stage, however, the Ottomans were just one among many beyliks. More powerful principalities existed, such as the Karamanids in central Anatolia. The question was why the Ottoman Beylik—initially smaller in size—would eventually overshadow all others.

Economic and Geographic Advantages

One theory highlights geography: The Ottomans were located close to the Byzantine Empire's vulnerable frontiers. While this posed dangers, it also provided an avenue for expansion. Raids into Byzantine lands could yield wealth and resources, attracting more followers to the Ottoman banner. As Byzantine power waned, the Ottomans increasingly found themselves in possession of strategic fortresses and trade routes.

Another factor was the region's population dynamics. Western Anatolia had faced waves of migration and conflict, leading to depopulation in some areas.

When Ottomans captured new territories, they needed to settle them with loyal populations. Over time, they cultivated a reputation for relative tolerance. Local Greek and Armenian populations might find Ottoman rule less oppressive than expected, especially if local taxes were set at a manageable level and if religious leaders were given certain protections. This pragmatic approach helped the Ottomans stabilize newly won areas.

The Question of Identity

From the outset, the small community around Osman was not solely Turkish. There was a mix of converts, local Christians, and Sufi dervishes who adhered to various brotherhoods. People in this region often switched allegiances based on opportunity and security. The Ottoman identity would gradually crystallize around the family of Osman, but in these early days, it was not clearly separate from other beyliks. Only through continued military success and skillful leadership would the Ottoman line begin to stand out.

Mongol Pressure and the Collapse of Seljuk Authority

Another reason the Ottomans were able to rise was the partial vacuum left by the Seljuk collapse. While the Mongols (through their Ilkhanate in Persia) had a presence in eastern Anatolia, their reach was not as strong in the western frontier zones. This relative distance from Mongol influence allowed frontier beys more independence. The Karamanids, Germiyanids, Aydınids, and other principalities jockeyed for power. Yet, over time, the Ottomans proved adept at pitting rivals against each other. Through strategic marriages and alliances, they expanded both eastward among Turkish beyliks and westward against the Byzantines.

The Legacy of Ertuğrul

Ertuğrul himself remains a semi-legendary figure. Early Ottoman chronicles, written generations later, often romanticized his deeds. While modern historians might question certain details, Ertuğrul clearly played a pivotal role in establishing the nascent Ottoman community near Söğüt. His leadership ensured that his followers had both land to cultivate and opportunities for military expansion. By the time he died (sometime in the late 13th century), he had laid a foundation for his son Osman.

Transition to Osman

When Osman succeeded his father, he inherited a small but strategically placed principality. Most scholars place his accession in the 1280s or 1290s, though exact dates remain debated. Osman was quick to take advantage of Byzantine weaknesses. He led raids, seized small forts, and reportedly had a vision—now famous in Ottoman lore—of a tree growing from his chest that shaded the world, a metaphor for the empire's future greatness.

Stories such as this demonstrate how the Ottoman court, in later years, cultivated myths around the founder. It was important for a mighty empire to trace its origins to a blessed or divinely guided event. Historians note that such myths likely emerged well after Osman's life, but they do suggest the deep respect and reverence he commanded among his followers.

Frontier Society and Raiding Culture

Raiders played a huge role in the early Ottoman economy and social structure. Known as "ghazis," these warriors were motivated by both religious zeal (the concept of jihad or "ghaza" against non-Muslims) and by material gain. It was a turbulent time, and the boundaries between raiding, trade, and settlement were often blurry.

When Osman led his men against Byzantine outposts, success meant capturing booty—livestock, goods, and sometimes captives who could be ransomed or sold.

This in turn brought wealth into the Ottoman Beylik, funding further conquests or fortifications. It also increased Osman's prestige, drawing more warriors to fight under his banner. However, a key aspect that distinguished the Ottomans was their evolving approach to administering newly won lands. Instead of simply plundering and moving on, they established control, allowed local inhabitants to continue farming, and integrated them into an emerging socio-political structure.

Religious and Cultural Ties

The cultural environment of early Ottoman Anatolia was fluid. Many Christians converted to Islam, either out of genuine belief, social pressure, or to gain favor with the new rulers. Others remained Christian but served in the Ottoman administration or army. This phenomenon would become more evident in later centuries, but its seeds were planted early on.

The role of Sufi orders, such as the Mevlevi (founded by Jalal ad-Din Rumi) and others, must be mentioned. These orders had wide followings across Anatolia. Their teachings emphasized spirituality, devotion, and sometimes an inclusive view of faith that appealed to frontier societies. Scholars theorize that Osman and his successors maintained good relationships with local Sufi sheikhs, who encouraged their disciples to settle in Ottoman-controlled areas, thus bolstering the population base and giving religious legitimacy to Ottoman rule.

Women in Early Ottoman Society

There is limited documentation about the roles of women in this early period, but as in many Turkmen nomadic societies, women had relatively more freedom compared to some sedentary societies. They could be involved in managing family holdings, taking part in migrations, and even influencing tribal alliances through marriage. In legends, the mother of Osman or influential wives sometimes appear as wise counselors, though it is hard to verify the accuracy of these accounts. Nonetheless, the daily life of women likely involved agriculture, weaving, and household management, much as it did in other rural communities of the time.

Architectural Footprints

In these early years, architecture was modest. The Ottomans would become famous for grand mosques and public buildings in later centuries, but in the 13th century, they focused on fortifications and small mosques or masjids (prayer halls). Their capital at Söğüt was little more than a fortified town. Some local historians have identified early Ottoman structures like a small mosque attributed to either Ertuğrul or Osman. Over time, these small buildings would multiply, signifying growing wealth and the desire to showcase power.

Governance and Legal Structures

Administration in this period was a patchwork. Each village or tribe might still follow its own customary laws, while the overarching authority of the bey extended to collecting taxes or tribute and ensuring military service. The Ottoman approach combined Turkic, Persian, and Islamic legal practices, echoing their Seljuk predecessors. The concept of "Kanun" (secular law or sultanic decrees) would develop more fully under later sultans like Mehmed II and Suleiman the Magnificent. For now, leadership revolved around the personal authority of the bey, reinforced by loyalty, the spoils of war, and the distribution of fiefs.

Interactions with the Byzantine Empire

Osman's earliest raids targeted Byzantine fortifications and towns in Bithynia. Despite the region's historical significance, the Byzantine Empire at this time was a shadow of its former self. Civil wars, financial woes, and the Latin occupation of Constantinople (1204–1261) had weakened Byzantine defenses. Local governors, often with limited help from the central government, had to deal with the growing Ottoman threat. Some attempted alliances with other beyliks or mercenary bands, but these efforts yielded only temporary relief.

The most symbolic moments were the gradual capture of key Byzantine towns, such as Yenişehir, which allowed the Ottomans to encircle Bursa, setting the stage for its eventual fall. The creation of frontier "akhis" (brotherhoods of craftspeople and traders) also formed part of the socio-economic foundation. These brotherhoods often spanned religious lines and encouraged commerce, linking Ottoman lands with Byzantine-held regions.

Expansion and Internal Cohesion

One critical aspect was that, despite the frontier environment, the early Ottomans managed to maintain internal cohesion. While other beyliks frequently suffered from dynastic splits and rivalries, Osman's family held together. This unity was strengthened by a shared sense of mission—conquest of infidel lands—and by the spoils system that rewarded loyal followers.

In these years, Ottoman expansion was not yet guaranteed. Other beyliks, like the Karasid or Germiyanid, might have overshadowed the Ottomans if history had taken different turns. However, the Ottomans' strategic focus on Byzantine lands proved advantageous. Instead of expending energy fighting their fellow Muslim neighbors, Osman's followers primarily turned westward.

The Symbolism of the Dream

Later Ottoman chronicles mention a famous dream attributed to Osman, often called the "Tree Dream." The story goes that Osman dreamt he was lying beside a holy figure (sometimes identified as Sheikh Edebali), and from his body a tree arose, covering vast territories. Leaves, branches, and fruits spread across three continents. While it is almost certainly apocryphal or heavily embellished, it served to legitimize Osman's claim to leadership and the empire's eventual destiny. Many dynasties in history have used such origin myths to portray divine favor. The dream narrative continued to be retold to reinforce the sultan's authority as the empire grew.

The Year 1300: A Snapshot

The turn of the century around 1300 found the Ottoman Beylik still quite modest in size. It was centered around Söğüt, with small expansions toward the Sakarya River and into Byzantine Bithynia. Osman was likely in his forties or fifties. The beylik's population consisted of Turkmen tribes, local Christians who had accepted Ottoman authority, and a growing number of tradespeople. It was a dynamic environment. Raiding parties were constantly probing Byzantine defenses, while the bey also managed diplomatic ties with other Turkish principalities to the east.

In the grand scheme of medieval Anatolia, the Ottomans were not the most powerful, but their star was rising. The key difference lay in their boldness against Byzantium and their ability to consolidate gains effectively.

Final Thoughts on Early Development

This early phase reveals the fundamental elements that shaped the Ottomans' future: frontier warfare, pragmatic administration, and the blending of various cultural influences. Even at this stage, we see a willingness to incorporate different ethnic and religious groups under Ottoman rule, a trend that would become a hallmark of the empire in later centuries.

While specifics of these early years are elusive, the broad narrative shows a tenacious and opportunistic beylik that gradually outpaced its rivals. By the time Osman took center stage, he was ready to lay claim to a legacy that would stretch far beyond the rolling hills of Bithynia.

With that, we complete our exploration of the 13th-century origins that set the stage for the Ottoman Empire. In the next chapter, we will focus on **Osman I** himself—his leadership style, key victories, and the administrative seeds he planted. This period will see the transformation of a minor frontier beylik into a more recognized political entity that caught the attention of neighbors and foes alike.

CHAPTER 2

THE RISE OF OSMAN I AND ESTABLISHMENT OF THE OTTOMAN BEYLIK

In this chapter, we delve deeper into the life and achievements of Osman I, the man traditionally recognized as the founder of the Ottoman Empire. Building upon the context established in Chapter 1, we will examine how Osman's strategic moves and leadership style helped transform a modest frontier group into a recognizable political power in northwestern Anatolia. This chapter covers the late 13th to early 14th centuries, focusing on Osman's consolidation of power, key battles against the Byzantines, and the socio-political structures he began to formalize.

Early Rule and Challenges

Osman likely took over leadership in the 1280s or 1290s, though exact dates are debatable due to limited contemporary sources. When Ertuğrul died, Osman inherited the small territory around Söğüt and Domaniç. At first, his claim to leadership may have been contested by other family members or by leading tribal figures, but the emerging consensus in the chronicles is that Osman's personal charisma and military prowess gained him wide support.

The environment was rife with possibility. The Byzantine Empire was still recovering from the Latin occupation of Constantinople (which ended in 1261) and facing internal disputes. Local Byzantine governors scrambled to defend their remaining territories in Bithynia, but they often lacked sufficient troops or resources. This situation presented Osman with an opening to expand at the Byzantines' expense.

The Battle of Bapheus (1302)

One of the earliest recorded military engagements involving Osman is the Battle of Bapheus, fought in 1302 near Nicomedia (modern-day İzmit). Chroniclers differ on the details, but it appears that a Byzantine force, possibly under the command of George Mouzalon, clashed with Ottoman raiders. The Ottomans emerged victorious, marking their first major defeat of a Byzantine field army. This victory had significant consequences:

1. **Boosted Reputation**: News of the victory would have spread among the Turkmen beyliks, heightening Osman's prestige and attracting more warriors to his banner.
2. **Territorial Gain**: The victory opened up more of the surrounding region to Ottoman raids and eventual conquest. It further isolated Byzantine outposts in Anatolia.
3. **Psychological Impact**: The Byzantines began to see the Ottoman threat as serious. The loss underscored the empire's weakened state, both financially and militarily.

Though the battle might not have been a large-scale clash by later standards, it was symbolic of the changing power dynamics in western Anatolia.

Osman's Leadership Qualities

From what we can glean, Osman demonstrated several qualities that contributed to his success:

1. **Diplomatic Skill**: He secured alliances or neutrality with some neighboring beyliks, ensuring he could focus on the Byzantine frontier without constant distractions from the east.
2. **Religious Legitimation**: By aligning himself with influential Sufi sheikhs like Edebali, Osman gained moral and spiritual support. This connection strengthened his appeal among the devout Turkmen.

3. **Flexible Administration**: He began adopting aspects of the Seljuk administrative framework where useful, but remained pragmatic, allowing local customs to continue if they ensured stability.
4. **Inclusiveness**: Even at this early stage, the Ottomans showed a pattern of accommodating local populations. This approach would later help them govern vast territories with diverse cultures.

Although it is tempting to attribute all these qualities to Osman personally, it is equally possible that the early Ottoman leadership was a collective effort. Even so, Ottoman chronicles place Osman at the heart of every major decision, reflecting the later empire's emphasis on a single dynastic line.

Siege of Bursa and Regional Conquests

With the Byzantines in retreat, Osman turned his sights on more ambitious targets. Bursa (in Turkish, "Bursa" or historically "Brusa") was a key city in the region. Its capture would grant access to trade routes, wealth, and a more permanent urban center than the countryside forts. The siege of Bursa likely began in the early 1300s but was a protracted affair, as Osman's forces lacked the means for a swift capture. Instead, they employed blockade tactics, cutting off supply lines and slowly wearing down the city's defenders.

By some accounts, Bursa fell around 1326, although historical accuracy regarding the exact date is tricky. It seems Osman did not personally see the city's final surrender, as he died around that time. Regardless, Bursa's eventual capture became a milestone. Under Osman and, more definitively, under his son Orhan, Bursa transformed into the first major Ottoman capital.

During this period, the Ottomans also took smaller forts in the region, consolidating their grip on Bithynia. The steady accumulation of territory gave them credibility as a formidable power rather than just another roving band of ghazis.

Administrative Seeds

Though the empire's famous institutions—like the devşirme system or the centralized bureaucracy—had not yet emerged, the seeds of future governance were being planted. Osman entrusted local rulership to loyal commanders (beys), who received lands (timars) in exchange for military service. This arrangement fostered loyalty and secured a measure of local order.

Simultaneously, the Ottomans began establishing rudimentary courts to handle disputes among the Muslim population, using a combination of Islamic law (Sharia) and customary practices. Non-Muslim subjects were often allowed to follow their own religious laws in personal matters, as long as they paid the jizya (a tax on non-Muslims). This system, which would become more formal in later centuries, reflected the early Ottoman approach of flexibility and pragmatism.

Myth vs. Reality

Modern historians caution that much of what we know about Osman is colored by later Ottoman historians seeking to glorify the dynasty's founder. Stories of miraculous victories, prophecies, and saintly lineage must be read critically. However, there is no doubt that, under Osman's guidance, the small principality in Söğüt evolved into a dynamic force challenging the Byzantine presence in Anatolia.

The Legacy of Osman

As noted, Osman likely passed away around 1323–1324 or perhaps as late as 1326. By that time, the Ottomans were on the verge of a new era. While historians debate whether Osman or his son Orhan can be credited with certain conquests, it is beyond dispute that Osman's tenure set the trajectory. He established:

- **A coherent leadership structure** under a single ruling family.
- **A warrior ethos** that emphasized the ghazi spirit, appealing to Turkmen fighters.

- **A growing administrative sense** that balanced the demands of warfare with the necessity of stable governance.
- **A capital-in-the-making**: Bursa, eventually captured fully by Orhan, served as a tangible symbol of permanence. The environment should convey that this city is transitioning from Byzantine to Ottoman rule.

Socio-Religious Policies Under Osman

Though the term "millet system" is more commonly associated with later centuries, some rudimentary form of communal autonomy for religious groups can be traced back to the earliest Ottoman days. Christians and Jews under Ottoman authority were often left to manage their own affairs as long as they recognized the Ottoman ruler and paid taxes.

This religious tolerance, though pragmatic rather than purely ideological, helped the Ottomans integrate conquered populations without sparking major revolts. In a region long used to warfare and changing rulers, a policy that guaranteed a modicum of stability and respect for local customs could win hearts and minds—or at least reduce armed resistance.

Economic Growth and Trade

Even at this nascent stage, the Ottomans recognized the importance of trade. Northwestern Anatolia was a crossroads for merchants traveling between Europe, the Middle East, and the Black Sea. By securing roads and fortresses, Osman's forces made trade routes safer, encouraging commerce. Over time, the

Ottomans would control key ports and caravan routes, transforming them into essential commercial hubs.

Though in Osman's day, the economy remained largely agricultural, the foundations for a broader trade-based wealth accumulation were being laid. As the beylik expanded, it gained access to new markets and resources, fueling further military campaigns.

Relations with Neighboring Beyliks

At times, Osman allied with or married into neighboring beyliks. Matrimonial alliances were a common strategy; they bound different dynasties together, at least temporarily. While conflicts among Turkish beyliks continued, Osman's main focus remained the weakening Byzantine frontier. This avoided a war on two fronts and permitted steady territorial gains in Bithynia.

The Karamanid Beylik in central Anatolia was then one of the strongest. Yet, due to geopolitical reasons and their own conflicts, they did not immediately try to halt Osman's expansion westward. The Germiyanids, Aydınids, and Sarukhanids were similarly preoccupied. This environment granted Osman enough space to consolidate his holdings without facing a united Turkish opposition.

Cultural Synthesis

A hallmark of the later Ottoman Empire was its cultural fusion—Turkic, Byzantine, Persian, Arab, and others. The beginnings of that synthesis can be seen under Osman. As Byzantines were absorbed, some local customs intermingled with Ottoman practices. Greek-speaking Christians found themselves under Turkish governance, while the Ottomans adopted certain Byzantine administrative techniques, such as record-keeping and urban governance structures.

The process was slow and organic; frontier societies often experience significant cultural blending. Musicians, artisans, and traders from different backgrounds mingled in the markets of fledgling Ottoman towns. While the empire was not yet known for grand architectural achievements, modest examples of assimilation—such as the conversion of churches into mosques—could be found in newly captured areas.

Transition to Orhan

By the mid-1320s, Osman was either very old or had already passed away. His son Orhan gradually took the reins, overseeing the final phases of the Bursa siege. Upon its capture, Orhan made Bursa the empire's first capital, setting up the administrative apparatus that would guide future expansions. Some historians attribute the actual founding of the Ottoman dynasty more concretely to Orhan, considering Osman as the man who set the stage.

Nevertheless, Osman's symbolic importance is profound. The empire bore his name—"Osmanlı" in Turkish—emphasizing his role as the dynastic patriarch. Later generations looked back to Osman as the archetypal warrior-leader, forging an identity that resonated from the 14th century onward.

Lasting Impact of Osman's Era

Osman's era established core patterns:

1. **Continuous Territorial Growth**: Each generation aimed to expand, partly due to the ghazi mentality and partly due to economic incentives of conquests.
2. **Succession by Primogeniture**: Although Ottoman succession would grow complicated, the principle that Osman's lineage would rule was set.
3. **Flexible Tolerance**: Different faiths were allowed to operate under Ottoman supremacy, a major factor in the empire's longevity.
4. **Military-Administrative Synergy**: War provided resources, which in turn supported governance and further expansion.

These patterns would evolve, but the seeds were sown by Osman and his early circle of advisors, commanders, and religious supporters.

The Ghazi Ethos and Its Variations

"Ghazi" is a title carried with pride, denoting a warrior who fights in the name of Islam. However, many of these "holy warriors" were also motivated by material gain. Osman managed to harness this ethos without letting it splinter his realm into rival warbands, a delicate balance indeed. Some ghazis roamed independently, looking for loot wherever they could find it, whether it was Byzantine or even neighboring Muslim territory. By channeling their energies primarily against Byzantine lands, Osman offered them consistent opportunities for plunder and land grants.

Tribal Dynamics

Tribal allegiances in the 13th and early 14th centuries remained strong. Osman's base likely included various clans. Disputes or rivalries could arise over access to grazing land or control of trade routes. Yet the overarching impetus of conquest against Byzantium helped unify these tribes under a common goal. Still, some scholars posit that tensions would occasionally flare within the beylik, though these incidents are rarely detailed in surviving sources.

Bursa Before Ottoman Rule

Before the Ottomans, Bursa was a commercially vital town with connections to the Silk Road, albeit overshadowed by larger cities under Byzantine or other Turkish control. It boasted thermal springs that had attracted settlers for centuries. When Ottoman pressure increased, the city's economy suffered from repeated raids. Eventually, prolonged siege tactics forced Bursa into a capitulated surrender—likely with some terms permitting local notables to retain property or safe passage if they wished to leave. Once the city was firmly in Ottoman hands, it was systematically repopulated with a mix of Turkmen migrants, local Greeks who stayed, and other Muslim groups from surrounding regions.

Osman's Personal Life and Family

Ottoman chroniclers often mention Malhun Hatun (or Mal Hatun) as Osman's wife, though details vary. It is sometimes claimed she was the daughter of Sheikh Edebali, reinforcing a spiritual bond between the ruling family and religious leaders. Whether or not this is historically accurate, it served as a foundational myth for the dynasty's link to piety and learning.

Osman's known sons included Orhan, who succeeded him. There might have been other children, but records are sparse. Dynastic marriages later became strategic tools, but in Osman's time, alliances were more a matter of forging local ties within the region, merging the leadership circles of different clans or orders.

Symbolic Acts and Artifacts

Legends speak of Osman's sword (often referred to in later centuries as the Sword of Osman), a relic used in the coronation ceremonies of future sultans. While the authenticity of such an item is debated, the concept reflects the tradition of transferring authority via a physical symbol. Ottoman enthronement ceremonies for centuries would reference the legacy of Osman, using a special sword girding ceremony to formally acknowledge a new ruler's place in the dynastic line.

Reactions from the Byzantines

From the Byzantine perspective, Osman and his successors were initially seen as yet another wave of Turkmen raiders. Chroniclers lament the inability of the imperial government to muster resources to confront the growing threat effectively. Occasional attempts to form alliances with other Turkish beyliks against the Ottomans largely failed due to internal divisions. The Byzantine court in Constantinople was often embroiled in its own political intrigues, unable to mount a unified response until it was too late for many of its Anatolian holdings.

The End of an Era

By the time of Osman's death, the transition from a minor frontier group to a rising power was well underway. Even though the exact date and circumstances of Osman's passing are murky (some chroniclers say he died right before Bursa's fall; others suggest it was around the same time), it is clear that Orhan inherited an entity on the cusp of bigger conquests. Bursa, soon established as the Ottoman capital, became the seat of government, offering more sophisticated administrative possibilities than Söğüt ever could.

Osman's final resting place, according to tradition, is in Bursa, in a tomb (türbe) that was once part of a Byzantine church. This symbolic appropriation of a Byzantine religious site for the tomb of the Ottoman founder illustrates how the Ottomans integrated, repurposed, and layered their sovereignty over inherited institutions and structures. Later sultans would pay their respects at Osman's tomb, reinforcing the continuity of dynastic identity.

CHAPTER 3

EXPANSION UNDER ORHAN AND MURAD I

In this chapter, we follow the transformation of the Ottoman Beylik from a small principality into a significant power that caught the attention of neighboring states in both Anatolia and southeastern Europe. Under Orhan (Osman I's son) and later Murad I (Orhan's son), the Ottomans conquered major cities, organized a more structured administration, and moved across the Dardanelles into Thrace. These achievements marked a turning point in Ottoman history, laying strong foundations for further expansion in the centuries ahead.

1. ORHAN'S ACCESSION AND EARLY REFORMS

Orhan Succeeds Osman

Osman I, having spent most of his life building the beylik, left behind a growing realm centered in northwestern Anatolia. When Osman died (likely around 1323–1324 or shortly before the final capture of Bursa in 1326), Orhan inherited leadership. Orhan is often recognized as the first to take the title "Sultan" in some contemporary documents, although this was still a transitional period, and formal titles were less rigid than in later centuries.

Orhan's primary task was to build on his father's accomplishments. At the start of Orhan's rule, the Ottoman domain included Söğüt, Yenişehir, small forts in Bithynia, and the newly won city of Bursa. Although the Ottomans had steadily grown in strength, they were still far from the might they would achieve later. The young ruler had to consolidate recent conquests, bring stability to his new capital of Bursa, and secure additional territories that would cement Ottoman power in the region.

The Capture and Development of Bursa

Bursa's fall, completed under Orhan's watch, was a crucial event. Previously a Byzantine stronghold, it became the Ottomans' first major urban center and capital. Bursa offered many advantages:

1. **Economic Prosperity**: Bursa was known for its silk production and trade connections. By securing this city, the Ottomans tapped into profitable silk routes, which enriched the beylik's treasury.
2. **Strategic Location**: Situated near other Byzantine outposts like Nicaea (İznik) and Nicomedia (İzmit), Bursa served as a base for further expansion. It also allowed better control of the roads linking the Sea of Marmara to inland Anatolia.
3. **Symbolic Victory**: Conquering a well-known Byzantine city boosted Ottoman prestige among other beyliks and potential recruits.

Orhan invested in the city's development by encouraging trade, building mosques, and establishing charitable foundations (waqfs). These projects not only beautified Bursa but also served as a means of garnering local support. By improving commerce and civic life, Orhan strengthened his grip on the region.

Administrative Steps and the First Ottoman Coin

Orhan is often credited with introducing important administrative changes that would shape the state. Though small in scale compared to later reforms, these measures laid the groundwork for the empire's future governance.

- **Coinage**: One of Orhan's major innovations was the minting of the first Ottoman coins (akçe). Having a standardized currency helped promote trade and demonstrated the Ottomans' growing sense of political legitimacy. While other beyliks also minted coins, Orhan's coinage helped unify the Ottoman economy.

- **Military Organization**: Orhan recognized the importance of a standing military. Though the famous Janissary corps would appear in a more formal way under Murad I, the roots of a trained infantry were planted during Orhan's reign. He also maintained a cavalry force made up of frontier warriors (akıncı) and timar-holding horsemen.

With these steps, Orhan moved the Ottomans away from a purely tribal structure. The new administrative framework was modest at first, but it showed a willingness to adopt and adapt from Seljuk, Byzantine, and Persian models where beneficial.

2. CONQUESTS IN NORTHWESTERN ANATOLIA

Taking Nicaea (İznik)

After securing Bursa, Orhan set his sights on other Byzantine cities in the region. Nicaea (modern-day İznik) was historically important for both the Byzantine Empire and the Christian church, having hosted major councils. By the early 14th century, Nicaea's defenses were weakened by repeated conflicts. Orhan's campaign involved a mix of raids, diplomacy, and siege tactics. The Ottoman forces eventually captured the city around 1331.

The fall of Nicaea further fractured Byzantine power in northwestern Anatolia. For the Ottomans, it was a major victory. Orhan oversaw repairs to the city walls, encouraged Muslim and Christian inhabitants to return, and established some of the earliest Ottoman educational institutions. İznik became a cultural hub, symbolizing the growing sophistication of the Ottoman state.

Taking Nicomedia (İzmit)

Shortly after, Orhan focused on Nicomedia (present-day İzmit). This city was closer to Constantinople and gave the Ottomans control over a key port on the Gulf of İzmit. Its capture around 1337 tightened Ottoman dominance in the region, leaving only a handful of Byzantine outposts in northwestern Anatolia. At this point, the Ottomans were well on their way to fully encircling Constantinople's immediate hinterland, though the imperial capital itself remained too large a prize to conquer at that time.

Relations with Other Beyliks

As Orhan expanded westward, he was careful about his eastern flank. The Karamanids, Germiyanids, and other principalities still held significant power in central and southern Anatolia. Orhan managed these relations through marriage alliances, trade agreements, and occasional shows of force. Unlike some beyliks that became bogged down in internal disputes, the Ottomans under Orhan stayed focused on taking advantage of Byzantine weakness.

At times, Orhan also offered safe havens to Byzantine refugees or worked out ransom deals for captured nobles. These actions underscored the Ottomans' pragmatic approach: forging short-term truces or alliances when useful, but continuing their overall strategy of territorial expansion whenever an opportunity arose.

3. DIPLOMATIC MARRIAGES AND CROSS-BOSPORUS INFLUENCE

Marriage Alliances

Perhaps one of Orhan's most notable political moves was his marriage to Theodora, the daughter of John VI Kantakouzenos, a Byzantine noble who later became Emperor (reigning in Constantinople during a turbulent civil war). This marriage alliance demonstrated the complex dynamics of the region. While

Byzantium and the Ottomans were often at war, they occasionally worked together if it suited their interests.

Such diplomatic marriages had several effects:

1. **Temporary Peace**: They offered a respite from hostilities, at least in certain border regions.
2. **Cultural Exchange**: Individuals from Byzantine aristocratic circles became part of the Ottoman court, and vice versa, leading to some exchange of customs.
3. **Political Leverage**: The Ottomans could leverage familial ties to influence internal Byzantine affairs, especially during civil strife.

First Ottoman Foothold in Europe?

During Orhan's reign, Ottoman forces were invited to help in Byzantine conflicts. Some historians point to these interventions as the start of Ottoman influence in Thrace, though a permanent presence on European soil was not achieved until later. At this point, Ottoman soldiers were often used as mercenaries or allies by rival Byzantine factions. Each intervention familiarized the Ottomans with the region, setting the stage for future crossings into Gallipoli and beyond.

Trade Relations

As the Ottomans grew stronger in northwestern Anatolia, trade became an essential tool for both wealth and diplomacy. Genoese and Venetian merchants, already active in the area, sought commercial privileges from Orhan. In return, they provided ships or trade connections that benefited the Ottomans. Over time, the Ottoman port towns on the Sea of Marmara and the Aegean began to see more merchant traffic. This economic interplay would later accelerate under Murad I and subsequent sultans.

4. TRANSITION TO MURAD I

Orhan's Later Years

Orhan ruled for about 36 years (1326–1362, though some dates vary). During his tenure, the Ottoman beylik quadrupled in size, stabilizing itself as a regional power. In his later years, Orhan dealt with family rivalries, typical of dynastic politics, but he remained relatively successful in containing any serious internal challenge.

Though Orhan's health declined over time, he is remembered for laying down the organizational skeleton of the state. He passed on to his successor an entity that was financially stable, administratively functional, and militarily capable.

Murad I Takes the Throne

Upon Orhan's death, his son Murad ascended to the throne (around 1362). Murad inherited not a fragile border beylik but a substantial power in western Anatolia. From the start of his rule, Murad I showed strong military ambitions in the Balkans. Though the Ottomans would still face challenges to their east, Murad focused primarily on Europe, believing that long-term growth lay across the waters in Thrace and beyond.

---

5. EARLY BALKAN CAMPAIGNS UNDER MURAD I

The Strategic Value of Gallipoli

The first permanent Ottoman foothold in Europe came with the capture of Gallipoli (Gelibolu) in 1354, actually toward the end of Orhan's reign. An earthquake had damaged the city's walls, and the Ottomans, under Süleyman Pasha (Orhan's son), quickly moved to occupy it. When Murad took power, he recognized Gallipoli as a vital base for launching more campaigns in Thrace.

By having Gallipoli, the Ottomans no longer depended solely on Byzantine naval permissions to cross into Europe. They controlled their own crossing point. This shift was monumental: from that moment onward, the Ottomans steadily reinforced their presence in southeastern Europe.

Edirne (Adrianople) as a New Capital

Murad's ambitions in the Balkans became clear when Ottoman forces captured Adrianople (Edirne) in 1369, though some sources suggest an earlier date. Adrianople, an important city located in Thrace, became a practical base for operations deeper into Europe. Murad eventually designated Edirne as the Ottoman capital, signifying a shift in focus. With Bursa serving as a key capital in Anatolia, Edirne symbolized the empire's new European presence.

Establishing Edirne as a capital also aided in administering newly conquered Balkan territories. Ottoman governors and soldiers had a convenient seat of power from which to control the region.

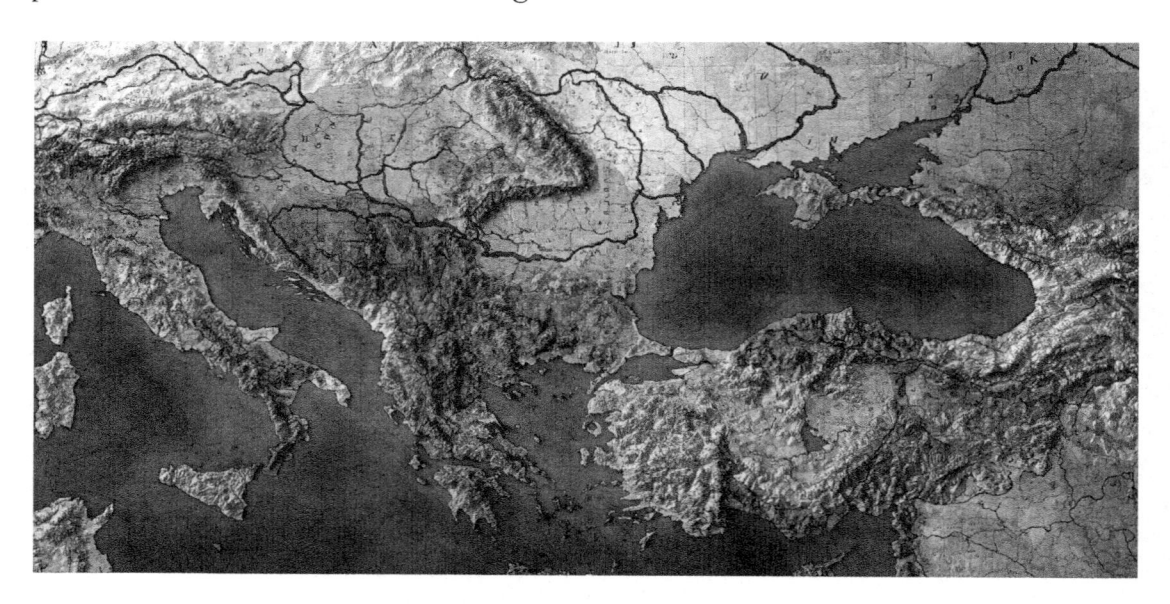

Opponents in the Balkans

The Balkan peninsula was a patchwork of principalities and kingdoms. Powers included the Bulgarian Tsardom, the Serbian Empire (though it was fracturing after the death of Stefan Dušan), the remnants of the Byzantine Empire in Thrace, and various smaller states like Wallachia and Bosnia. Murad's expansion threatened all of these. Sometimes they formed coalitions to resist the Ottomans, and sometimes local rulers allied with the Ottomans for personal gain. This fluid situation gave Murad chances to divide and conquer.

Examples of key confrontations:

- The Battle of Maritsa (1371), near the Maritsa River, where Ottoman forces defeated a Serbian-Bulgarian coalition.
- Minor skirmishes in the Rhodope Mountains and around Macedonia, allowing Murad to secure strategic fortresses.

Military Organization Under Murad

Murad I took steps to create a more disciplined standing army. While Orhan had begun this process, Murad expanded and formalized it. Among the most notable developments was the further institutionalization of the Janissaries—an elite infantry unit recruited through the devşirme system, which involved the conscription of Christian youths who were converted to Islam and trained as soldiers. In Murad's time, this system was still in its early stages, but it foreshadowed the powerful role the Janissaries would play in later centuries.

Additionally, Murad relied on:

- **Timar Cavalry**: Land grants given to soldiers (sipahis), who in turn provided military service.
- **Akıncı**: Irregular cavalry known for fast raids, crucial for softening up enemy territory.
- **Yaya**: Light infantry drawn from local populations.

Together, these forces gave the Ottomans flexibility and speed, key advantages in the fragmented Balkan landscape.

---

6. CONSOLIDATION IN ANATOLIA

Managing the Anatolian Front

While focused on the Balkans, Murad had to ensure stability in Anatolia. Rival beyliks, such as the Karamanids, continued to pose threats. At times, Murad led expeditions eastward to remind these beyliks of Ottoman power. Some were coerced into paying tribute or recognizing Ottoman suzerainty. Although these campaigns were not as high-profile as the Balkan ones, they were essential for maintaining the security of the empire's heartland.

Diplomacy and Marriage

Murad followed the example set by Orhan regarding diplomatic marriages. He sometimes married into other noble families or arranged marriages for his children to form temporary alliances. These ties helped quell unrest among certain Anatolian beys. In some cases, negotiations were backed by a clear demonstration of military might, ensuring that local rulers knew the price of defiance.

---

7. INTERNAL ADMINISTRATION AND SOCIAL STRUCTURE

Bureaucratic Growth

With territory expanding in both Anatolia and Europe, Murad needed a more elaborate bureaucracy. The old tribal methods of governance could not effectively manage diverse populations spread across vast distances. Drawing on Persian and Byzantine administrative traditions, the Ottomans developed a system where high-ranking officials (viziers) oversaw different departments, such as finance (defterdar) and the military (beylerbeyi).

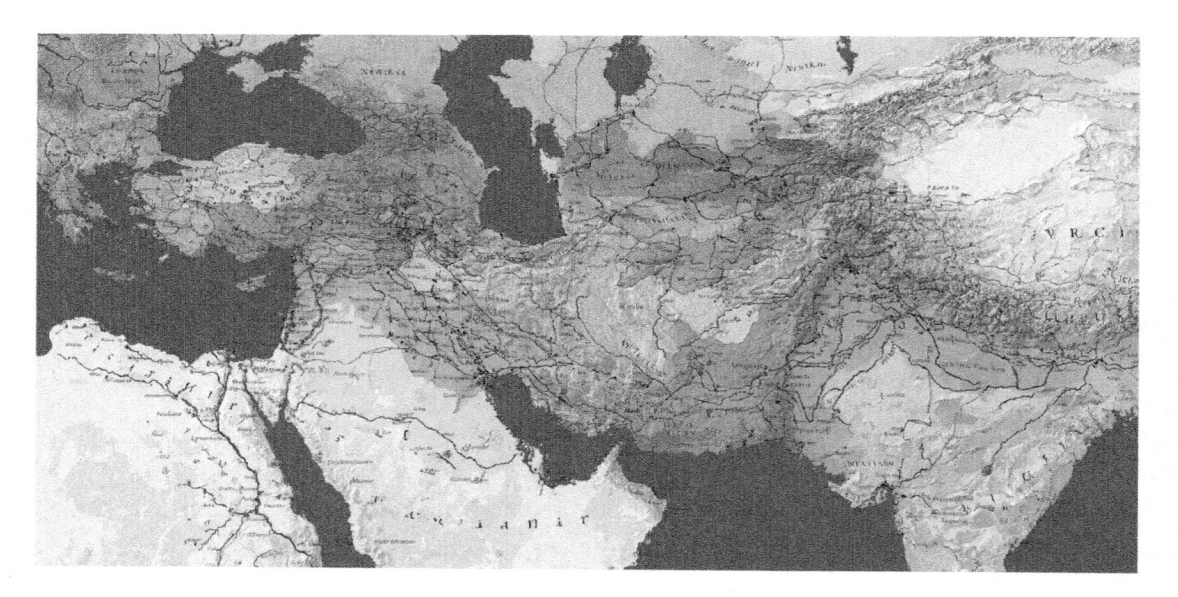

Records (defters) started to be kept more systematically, listing villages, taxpayers, and timar holders. This record-keeping improved tax collection and reduced corruption. It also helped the central government assess how many soldiers each timar-holding knight owed in time of war.

Religious Communities

By Murad's reign, the empire was home to various religious groups: Orthodox Christians in the Balkans, Armenian Christians in parts of Anatolia, Muslims of different backgrounds, and pockets of Jewish communities in major cities. The Ottomans continued their policy of relative tolerance, allowing non-Muslim communities to manage many of their own affairs. However, these groups paid additional taxes (like the jizya). This system, while it offered degrees of autonomy, also underscored that non-Muslims were second-class citizens in the empire. Still, the arrangement avoided large-scale rebellions, allowing the Ottomans to focus on external expansion.

Economic Dimensions

Trade routes crossing the empire enriched the treasury. With Edirne in Europe and Bursa in Anatolia, the Ottomans controlled key points between the East and West. Caravans carried spices, silk, and other goods through Ottoman lands. Murad encouraged this commerce by maintaining roads, protecting caravans, and offering tax incentives for merchants. The improved flow of trade increased state revenues, helping fund the standing army.

8. KEY MILITARY ENCOUNTERS AND THE RISE OF OTTOMAN PRESTIGE

The Battle of Maritsa (1371) in Detail

Sometimes called the Battle of Chernomen, this clash took place near the Maritsa River. A coalition of Serbian and Bulgarian forces attempted to stop the advancing Ottoman army but were caught off guard. Ottoman forces struck at night or early dawn, routing the coalition. This victory was important because it reduced Serbian influence south of the Balkans, opening more territory to Ottoman incursion. Many local lords chose to submit to Murad rather than risk total defeat.

Expansion into Macedonia and Bulgaria

Following Maritsa, Ottoman troops moved deeper into Macedonia, capturing fortresses and compelling local rulers to pay tribute. Skirmishes in Bulgaria led to the partial subjugation of the Bulgarian Tsardom, especially after the decline of Tarnovo. Some Bulgarian rulers tried to ally with Hungary or seek support from the Byzantine Emperor, but the Ottomans frequently outmaneuvered these attempts by offering better immediate terms or by exploiting local rivalries.

Implications for Europe

As Ottoman forces pressed into Europe, concerns grew among European powers. Some called for a new crusade. Venice, Genoa, and other maritime republics were less eager to commit to large-scale conflict, preferring to maintain trade relations with the Ottomans. Hungary and other states along the Danube border started to see the Ottoman presence as a direct threat This tension foreshadowed bigger conflicts to come, most notably in the late 14th and 15th centuries.

9. THE BATTLE OF KOSOVO (1389) AND ITS AFTERMATH

Prelude to Kosovo

By the late 1380s, Murad I had made significant inroads into Serbia and other Balkan territories. Serbian princes, notably Prince Lazar Hrebeljanović, sought to halt Ottoman expansion. They formed a broad alliance that included Bosnian and other regional leaders. The confrontation came to a head at the Battle of Kosovo in June 1389. This battle holds deep symbolic importance in the Balkans, even centuries later, but our focus remains on its historical outcome at the time.

The Battle Unfolds

Murad led a large Ottoman army into the Kosovo field. The opposing forces included Serbian heavy cavalry, infantry, and contingents from neighboring regions. Details of the battle are subject to later folklore, but generally:

1. **Initial Clashes**: The Serbian knights mounted strong charges, inflicting some casualties on the Ottoman front lines.
2. **Ottoman Counterattacks**: Ottoman archers and cavalry maneuvers managed to disrupt the Serbian ranks.
3. **Murad's Death**: At some point during or after the battle, Murad I was assassinated—some accounts say by a Serbian noble (Miloš Obilić). This event is wrapped in legend, but it is widely accepted that Murad was killed on or near the battlefield.
4. **Serbian Defeat**: Despite Murad's death, the Ottoman leadership (likely with Murad's son Bayezid) regrouped and won a decisive victory. Serbian forces suffered heavy losses, including Prince Lazar, who was captured and executed.

Consequences of Kosovo

- **Ottoman Consolidation**: Though the death of Murad could have caused chaos, the Ottomans quickly recognized Bayezid as the new ruler. The victory weakened Serbian power and paved the way for deeper Ottoman influence in the Balkans.
- **Legend and Memory**: The battle became a focal point of Serbian national identity, generating many myths and songs about heroism and betrayal. For the Ottomans, it was a testament to their unstoppable drive, though the loss of Murad tempered the celebration.
- **Transition of Power**: Bayezid took the throne at a critical moment, inheriting an empire that stretched across Anatolia and into southeastern Europe.

10. LEGACY OF ORHAN AND MURAD I

By the end of Murad I's reign, the Ottomans had transformed from a frontier beylik into a formidable regional empire. The shifts in power were dramatic:

1. **Territorial Expansion**: They controlled much of northwestern Anatolia, Thrace, Macedonia, and parts of Bulgaria and Serbia.
2. **Administrative Growth**: Systems for taxation, governance, and military organization were more refined.
3. **Cultural Impact**: Bursa, Edirne, and other cities saw the construction of mosques, schools, and public buildings, reflecting new Ottoman wealth and ambition.
4. **Dynastic Legitimacy**: With victories over rivals like the Byzantine Empire and various Balkan states, the Ottoman ruling family solidified its claims to rule over diverse populations.

Orhan's long reign established a stable base, while Murad's victories in the Balkans and Anatolia proved the empire's military might. This momentum set the stage for the next significant phase under Bayezid I, who inherited both the resources and the challenges left by Murad's death at Kosovo.

CHAPTER 4

BAYEZID I AND THE TIMURID INVASION

In this chapter, we delve into the reign of Bayezid I—often called Bayezid the Thunderbolt (Yıldırım). He inherited an expanding empire that spanned Anatolia and the Balkans, holding great promise but also facing serious challenges. Bayezid is known for his swift campaigns against rival beyliks, his clashes with European powers, and his fateful encounter with Timur (Tamerlane), the Central Asian conqueror. The events of his reign would shape Ottoman history for decades, especially after the devastating outcome at the Battle of Ankara in 1402.

1. BAYEZID I'S RISE TO POWER

Immediate Challenges After Kosovo

Bayezid came to power under extraordinary circumstances. His father, Murad I, had been killed during or immediately after the Battle of Kosovo (1389). Even though the Ottomans won that battle, they faced potential instability. Bayezid moved quickly to secure his throne, reputedly ordering the execution of his younger brother to eliminate any succession disputes—a brutal but not uncommon practice in the Ottoman tradition.

Despite the shock of Murad's death, the Ottoman administrative system helped maintain continuity. Commanders and provincial governors recognized Bayezid's authority, allowing him to focus on external threats rather than internal dissent. He returned to Edirne to confirm his position, then swiftly resumed expansionist policies.

Bayezid's Leadership Style

Bayezid I was known for his energy and speed in warfare—hence the nickname "the Thunderbolt." He also had a reputation for impatience and anger. Chronicles from his time mention that he was fiercely determined, often driving his armies across vast distances in quick, surprise attacks. This approach brought rapid victories but could also stretch Ottoman resources.

Under Bayezid's direction, the military structures begun under Orhan and Murad grew further. The Janissaries formed the core of the infantry, while sipahi cavalry continued to serve under the timar system. Bayezid also maintained relationships with akıncı raiders, who helped soften up enemy territories before the main army's arrival.

---

2. CONSOLIDATION AND CENTRALIZATION IN ANATOLIA

Subjugating Other Turkish Beyliks

From the moment he took power, Bayezid aimed to bring all the Turkish beyliks in Anatolia under his direct control. Previous sultans had sometimes tolerated the semi-independent existence of these smaller states, focusing instead on the Byzantine frontier. Bayezid, by contrast, believed a unified Anatolia was essential for Ottoman security and prosperity.

Key targets included:

- **The Karamanids** (centered around Konya), who were longtime rivals and had previously challenged Ottoman authority.
- **The Germiyanids, Aydınids, Sarukhanids, and Menteşe** beyliks in western Anatolia, which had alliances or rivalries with the Ottomans.

Through a mix of diplomacy and force, Bayezid quickly annexed many of these territories. Some beyliks recognized the strength of the Ottomans and surrendered in return for local autonomy or positions within the Ottoman administration. Others resisted, leading to short but intense military campaigns.

Centralizing Administration

One outcome of these campaigns was the rapid expansion of Ottoman governance into the heart of Anatolia. Bayezid placed Ottoman governors (beys or sancakbeys) in conquered areas, introduced the timar system to reward loyal soldiers, and collected taxes more effectively. This move towards centralization was a significant departure from earlier practices, where local leaders retained substantial autonomy. Bayezid believed that strong central authority would make the Ottomans more formidable and ensure a steady flow of revenue for his military ambitions.

---

3. CLASHES WITH EUROPEAN POWERS

Tensions in the Balkans

While Bayezid was centralizing Anatolia, he did not neglect the Balkans. The Ottomans already controlled large parts of Thrace, Macedonia, and Bulgaria. Serbian princes, though weakened by the Battle of Kosovo, remained in the region. Some had become Ottoman vassals. Others tried to organize resistance, often seeking aid from Hungary or other Christian powers.

Bayezid launched campaigns to solidify control. In 1390 and the early 1390s, Ottoman armies pressed deeper into Serbian territories and threatened the lands near the Danube. Some Bulgarian strongholds also came under firmer Ottoman rule during these operations.

Siege of Constantinople (1394–1402)

One of Bayezid's most ambitious moves was to lay siege to Constantinople itself. The Byzantine Empire by this time was a fraction of its former strength, essentially limited to the city and its immediate surroundings. The Ottomans encircled the walls, cutting off supplies and aiming to starve the city into submission. However, Constantinople's strong defenses and a late arrangement for aid from European powers prolonged the siege. Even though Bayezid's blockade caused great hardship inside the city, the Ottomans could not force an outright surrender.

The Crusade of Nicopolis (1396)

Growing alarm in Europe over Bayezid's aggressions led to calls for a crusade. Led primarily by King Sigismund of Hungary and joined by French, Burgundian, and other European knights, the crusade aimed to break Ottoman power in the Balkans. The confrontation came at the Battle of Nicopolis, located in present-day Bulgaria, on the Danube River.

- **Outcome**: The Ottomans won a decisive victory. European knights, overconfident and disorganized, suffered a crushing defeat. Many were captured or killed.
- **Aftermath**: Bayezid's triumph at Nicopolis bolstered his reputation as a champion of Islam and a formidable leader. It also weakened the last vestiges of resistance among Balkan states, and some local rulers rushed to reaffirm vassal status to the Ottomans.
- **European Perspective**: The defeat shocked European courts and slowed further large-scale crusading efforts for a time.

The victory at Nicopolis solidified the Ottomans' hold in southeastern Europe, allowing Bayezid to increase pressure on Constantinople. However, just when the dream of capturing the Byzantine capital seemed within reach, a new threat emerged from the East: Timur (Tamerlane).

4. THE RISE OF TIMUR (TAMERLANE)

Timur's Background

Timur, often known in the West as Tamerlane, was a Turco-Mongol conqueror from Central Asia. Rising out of the chaos that followed the decline of the Mongol Empire, Timur established a vast domain centered in Transoxiana (modern Uzbekistan). He claimed to be the restorer of Genghis Khan's legacy, though he was not a direct descendant. Known for his ruthless tactics and strategic brilliance, Timur created a fearsome army that conquered large parts of Persia, Mesopotamia, the Caucasus, and beyond.

By the late 1390s, Timur turned his attention to the western fringe of his empire, looking at the Middle East and Anatolia. Conflict with the Ottomans seemed almost inevitable because Bayezid's expansions in Anatolia had diminished or replaced the smaller beyliks, some of which asked Timur for protection or intervention.

Conflicting Interests in Anatolia

Timur was a master at exploiting rivalries. Many Anatolian beyliks that Bayezid had annexed or forced into submission began appealing to Timur for help. They depicted Bayezid as an upstart threatening the old Turkish order. Timur, always seeking new conquests, wrote letters to Bayezid demanding respect and deference. Bayezid refused to bow, insulting Timur in his correspondence.

As a result, Timur began to move westward, securing his positions in Persia and northern Mesopotamia. By 1400, he was poised to challenge Bayezid's control over eastern Anatolia. Meanwhile, Bayezid was still partially focused on besieging Constantinople, believing that the city would soon fall. Underestimating Timur's threat would prove to be a critical mistake.

5. THE BATTLE OF ANKARA (1402)

Prelude to the Clash

In 1400–1401, Timur sacked parts of Syria (which was under Mamluk control) and advanced into eastern Anatolia, capturing the city of Sivas—an important Ottoman fortress. Bayezid scrambled to respond, pulling back some forces from Constantinople and the Balkans. The two armies finally met near Ankara in July 1402. The site was chosen partly because Timur had advanced so far without significant Ottoman resistance, and Bayezid felt compelled to confront him there.

Composition of the Armies

- **Ottoman Army**: Bayezid's forces included Janissaries, sipahi cavalry, vassal contingents from the Balkans, and troops from Anatolia. Morale was mixed; some Anatolian troops resented Bayezid's harsh centralization.

- **Timurid Army**: Timur's forces were experienced veterans who had fought in multiple campaigns across Asia. They included heavy cavalry, skilled horse archers, and siege engineers. Timur also had the support of some local Anatolian beys who despised Bayezid's rule.

Course of the Battle

Accounts vary, but most agree on the following sequence:

1. **Initial Engagement**: Bayezid's forces attacked aggressively. However, the heat of the Anatolian summer and the exhaustion from forced marches took a toll on the Ottomans.
2. **Defections**: Crucially, some Anatolian beylik contingents under Bayezid switched sides mid-battle or fled, undermining the Ottoman battle line.
3. **Timurid Maneuvers**: Timur's cavalry outflanked the Ottomans, surrounding them and cutting off their supply lines.
4. **Bayezid's Capture**: After hours of fierce fighting, the Ottoman lines collapsed. Bayezid was captured by Timur's forces, a shocking blow to Ottoman prestige.

Aftermath and Consequences

The Battle of Ankara was disastrous for the Ottomans:

- **Loss of the Sultan**: With Bayezid taken prisoner, the empire faced a power vacuum.
- **Civil War**: Bayezid's sons vied for control, plunging the Ottomans into a period of turmoil known as the Interregnum (1402–1413).
- **Freed Beyliks**: Many of the Anatolian beyliks that Bayezid had subdued regained independence under Timur's protection.
- **Timur's Return East**: Interestingly, Timur did not attempt to permanently occupy Anatolia. He installed or recognized local rulers, then returned to Central Asia to pursue other campaigns. His timing, however, left the Ottomans in chaos.

---

6. IMPACT OF THE TIMURID INVASION

Collapse of Ottoman Authority in Anatolia

After Ankara, the beyliks of Karaman, Germiyan, and others quickly threw off Ottoman control. Even areas that stayed nominally loyal to the Ottomans faced confusion, as local governors did not know which son of Bayezid to recognize as the legitimate ruler. Important cities like Bursa and Edirne remained under Ottoman control in name, but leadership varied as Bayezid's sons fought among themselves.

Bayezid's Imprisonment and Death

Bayezid died in captivity around 1403. Rumors and stories about his final days spread through both Muslim and Christian lands. Some chroniclers painted Timur as a cruel jailor, while others indicated that Bayezid's spirit was broken by the defeat. Regardless of the circumstances, the sultan's death ended any hope that a single strong figure might quickly reunite the empire.

European and Byzantine Reactions

In Europe, news of the Ottoman defeat was met with relief, as the "Thunderbolt" who had crushed the crusaders at Nicopolis was no longer a threat. The siege of Constantinople was lifted, giving the Byzantine Empire a temporary reprieve. Some Balkan states also saw an opportunity to assert more independence or reclaim territory lost to the Ottomans. However, the region's future remained uncertain, as it was not clear which of Bayezid's sons—if any—could restore Ottoman strength.

---

7. THE BEGINNING OF THE INTERREGNUM

Ottoman Civil War (1402–1413)

With Bayezid's death, at least four of his sons claimed the throne:

- **Süleyman Çelebi**, based in Edirne, controlling much of the European side.
- **İsa Çelebi**, who tried to rule from Bursa.
- **Mehmed Çelebi**, based in Amasya, later known as Mehmed I.
- **Musa Çelebi**, who also held territory in Rumelia (the Balkan side).

Each prince received support from different factions, regions, or foreign powers. They fought against each other in battles across both Anatolia and the Balkans, causing destruction and instability. This period threatened to undo all the gains made since Orhan's time, and the empire came close to fragmenting permanently.

Timur's Disinterest in Long-Term Control

Timur's withdrawal from Anatolia meant that he did not establish a lasting empire in the region. He dismantled much of Bayezid's structure but did not replace it with a single Timurid administration. Instead, he allowed local rulers (some loyal to him, some not) to fight among themselves. This strategy was consistent with Timur's broader approach: conquer, loot, and weaken potential rivals without necessarily administering the conquered lands in a direct, long-term fashion.

---

8. LEGACY OF BAYEZID I

Despite his catastrophic defeat, Bayezid I left a lasting mark on Ottoman history:

1. **Rapid Expansion**: Under his leadership, the empire reached new heights in both Anatolia and the Balkans.
2. **Centralization Efforts**: He attempted to merge the beyliks into a single Ottoman state, setting a model for future sultans.
3. **Military Prowess**: Victories like Nicopolis cemented the Ottomans' reputation as a dominant military force in southeastern Europe.
4. **Overreach**: Bayezid's downfall highlights the dangers of rapid expansion without securing internal stability. His failure to address Anatolian resentment ultimately contributed to the defections at Ankara.
5. **Prelude to Renewal**: While the Interregnum threatened the empire's survival, the eventual victor—Mehmed I—would lay the foundations for a more stable Ottoman rule in the 15th century.

Contrasting Views on Bayezid

Contemporaries and later historians have debated Bayezid's legacy. Some admire his courage and skill, crediting him with nearly subduing Constantinople and unifying Anatolia. Others criticize him for hubris and impulsiveness, leading to the empire's near collapse. Nonetheless, he stands out as a pivotal figure whose reign both expanded the Ottoman world and exposed its vulnerabilities.

CHAPTER 5

THE INTERREGNUM AND THE RISE OF MEHMED I

When Sultan Bayezid I was defeated and captured by Timur at the Battle of Ankara in 1402, few could have imagined how close the Ottoman Empire came to disintegrating entirely. The empire that had expanded swiftly across Anatolia and the Balkans now found itself without a central guiding authority. Bayezid's sons, each claiming a right to the throne, descended into a bitter civil war that lasted over a decade. This chaotic period is known in Ottoman history as the **Fetret Devri** (the Interregnum). It was a time marked by shifting alliances, betrayals, and regional upheavals. Ultimately, it was Mehmed Çelebi—later known as Mehmed I—who emerged from the rubble to reunify the empire. This chapter explores the political, social, and military complexities of the Interregnum, as well as the rise of Mehmed I and his consolidation of power.

1. AFTERMATH OF THE BATTLE OF ANKARA

Immediate Disarray

The Battle of Ankara (1402) was a devastating blow. With Sultan Bayezid in Timur's custody, rumors spread rapidly throughout the empire. Soldiers and administrators alike worried about who would assume control. Unlike in previous successions, there was no designated heir apparent; several of Bayezid's sons held claims, each commanding different military units and administrative networks.

Timur, for his part, did not attempt a permanent occupation of the Ottoman heartlands. He dismantled much of Bayezid's authority in Anatolia by reinstating independent Turkish beyliks—Karaman, Germiyan, Aydın, and others—that Bayezid had forcibly annexed. With Ottoman power in apparent collapse, these beyliks reclaimed autonomy. Meanwhile, in the Balkans, local Christian rulers took advantage of the power vacuum to reassert independence or regain lost territories.

Political Fragmentation

Bayezid's sons, known in historical accounts as the **Çelebi princes**, included:

1. **Süleyman Çelebi** – Based primarily in Rumelia (the Balkans) with Edirne as his capital.
2. **İsa Çelebi** – Initially holding sway over Bursa and its environs in northwestern Anatolia.
3. **Musa Çelebi** – Involved in shifting alliances, sometimes controlling parts of Rumelia and sometimes moving back to Anatolia.
4. **Mehmed Çelebi** – Based in Amasya, in the eastern part of what had been Ottoman territory.

Each son had supporters—be they local notables, remnants of the Ottoman military, or foreign backers. The question was not only who could claim the throne but also who could effectively govern the fractured lands once ruled by Bayezid. For a decade, the empire was divided, with each son acting as a de facto ruler over his region.

---

2. PRINCE SÜLEYMAN ÇELEBI IN THE BALKANS

Early Advantage

Süleyman Çelebi initially emerged as one of the stronger contenders. He held the European side of the empire, a region still relatively intact after Ankara because Timur's forces had not crossed into the Balkans in large numbers. Moreover, the wealth of Rumelia's towns and the presence of established Ottoman garrisons allowed Süleyman to project power quickly.

From his base in Edirne, Süleyman opened diplomatic relations with the Byzantine Empire in Constantinople, neighboring Balkan principalities, and even Western European states. He sought to secure their recognition or at least their neutrality. In exchange for peace, he sometimes gave up certain territories or eased pressures on Constantinople, hoping to focus on eliminating rival claimants in Anatolia.

Governance Style

While Süleyman's rule showed promise—he continued to maintain the existing military structures and collected taxes effectively—he often faced criticism for his favoritism toward certain advisors and for his failure to unify the empire decisively. Moreover, the concessions he made to the Byzantines, including territory and tribute, caused resentment among other Ottoman factions who saw his diplomacy as capitulation.

---

3. PRINCE İSA ÇELEBİ AND BURSA

Control of the Ottoman Heartland

Shortly after Ankara, İsa Çelebi managed to occupy Bursa, the old Ottoman capital in Anatolia. Bursa held symbolic significance, having been the seat of Orhan and Murad I. In addition, it was economically important with its silk and textile industries. By holding Bursa, İsa gained legitimacy and a steady income from trade.

However, he faced stiff competition from his brothers. Mehmed Çelebi, who governed the Amasya region, posed the most significant threat. İsa was forced to devote resources to defending Bursa against Mehmed's expanding influence in the north and east.

Conflict with Mehmed

The struggle between İsa and Mehmed shaped the early years of the Interregnum in Anatolia. While the other princes fought for Rumelia, these two battled over the core Turkish lands. Several fierce engagements took place around Eskisehir and the plains of western Anatolia. Mehmed's tactical skill and alliances with local beyliks (initially wary of both Ottoman contenders) gave him a slight edge. After a series of defeats, İsa fled Bursa, eventually finding refuge with Süleyman in Rumelia.

---

4. PRINCE MUSA ÇELEBI: A WILD CARD

Entry into the Fray

Musa Çelebi emerged later than his brothers in claiming territory. Initially, he supported Süleyman in the Balkans. Over time, disputes arose, partly due to Musa's ambitions and partly due to Süleyman's refusal to share authority. A turning point came when Mehmed approached Musa with a plan: if Musa helped Mehmed undermine Süleyman's power in Rumelia, Mehmed would back Musa's claim there.

The Alliance with Mehmed

Following this agreement, Musa led an army into Rumelia to challenge Süleyman directly. The Balkan lords—some loyal to Süleyman, others open to new alliances—became pivotal. Eventually, Musa defeated Süleyman in battle. Süleyman fled toward Constantinople but was captured and killed, leaving Rumelia under Musa's control. However, this new arrangement soon led to a falling-out between Mehmed and Musa, as Musa began to assert greater autonomy.

---

5. MEHMED ÇELEBI: THE STEADY STRATEGIST

Base in Amasya

While his brothers scrambled for power in Edirne or Bursa, Mehmed's stronghold was Amasya, a region known for its strategic position and relative wealth. Amasya's mountainous terrain and loyal local administrators provided Mehmed with a secure base. He cultivated alliances with surviving beyliks, ensuring they would remain neutral or supportive in his conflicts with other Çelebi princes.

Mehmed's leadership style was measured. He avoided overextending himself, focusing on consolidating each new gain before moving on. Diplomacy played a large role. Mehmed placed local elites in positions of influence, ensuring their loyalty. He also carefully managed relations with outside powers like the Byzantines and the Karamanids, promising trade privileges or non-aggression pacts.

Gradual Expansion

Between 1405 and 1410, Mehmed methodically expanded from Amasya into surrounding territories, capturing towns and re-establishing the Ottoman administrative system that had collapsed after Ankara. Each victory weakened his rivals' positions. When İsa fled Bursa, Mehmed took control of the city, further solidifying his claim as the leading Ottoman ruler in Anatolia.

6. CONFRONTATIONS BETWEEN MEHMED AND MUSA

The Turning Point in Rumelia

After Musa toppled Süleyman in Rumelia, he declared himself the sole ruler of the Balkans. He pressured Byzantine outposts, attacked local lords who resisted, and sought to consolidate all of Rumelia under his authority. However, many Balkan nobles complained about Musa's harsh rule. They began to see Mehmed as a more moderate alternative who might restore a stable, predictable government.

Recognizing an opportunity, Mehmed crossed into Rumelia with an army. The two brothers clashed at several battles, the most decisive taking place around 1413 near the Vitosha Mountains in Bulgaria or possibly near modern-day Sofia. Mehmed emerged victorious, capturing and ultimately executing Musa. With Musa gone, Mehmed effectively ruled both the Balkans and large portions of Anatolia.

Byzantine Involvement

Throughout the Interregnum, the Byzantine Empire under Emperor Manuel II Palaiologos played a balancing act, sometimes supporting one Çelebi prince over another in the hopes of securing concessions. By 1413, with Mehmed triumphant, the Byzantines recognized him as the legitimate Ottoman sultan, hoping to maintain peace and preserve what remained of their territories. Mehmed, in turn, allowed Constantinople a respite from direct Ottoman aggression, at least temporarily.

---

7. MEHMED I'S CONSOLIDATION OF POWER

Diplomacy and Reconciliation

Emerging as the victor of the Interregnum, Mehmed I faced the colossal task of reuniting a fragmented empire. Many regions had grown used to autonomy—whether under rival princes or reinstated beyliks. Mehmed pursued a careful policy of reconciliation, offering amnesty to those who submitted, guaranteeing local rights, and reinstating certain former officials if they pledged loyalty.

He also negotiated with the Anatolian beyliks, some of which had allied with Timur and regained independence. Mehmed's approach was less punitive than Bayezid's had been; he incorporated these beyliks into the Ottoman fold more diplomatically, leveraging marriages, tributes, and local autonomy deals. Over time, this approach proved effective, and most of the beyliks either recognized Mehmed's overlordship or were absorbed with minimal resistance.

Central Administration Strengthening

To prevent future civil wars, Mehmed reinforced central structures:

- **Governance**: He placed trusted advisors and family members in key provinces.
- **Military**: He reorganized the Janissaries and timar cavalry, ensuring they remained loyal to the sultan rather than to individual princes.
- **Finance**: Recovery from the devastation of the civil war required efficient tax collection and trade revival. Mehmed supported the reopening of caravan routes and provided incentives for merchants to come back to Ottoman markets.

He also sought to restore the public's faith in Ottoman rule. Mosque-building projects and the reconstruction of markets and caravanserais symbolized the return of stability. Intellectual and religious figures were encouraged to settle in Ottoman cities, signaling that the empire was once again open for cultural and scholarly pursuits.

8. REGIONAL CHALLENGES AND REBELLIONS

The Sheikh Bedreddin Revolt

One of the most notable challenges to Mehmed I's rule was the rebellion led by **Sheikh Bedreddin** (Şeyh Bedreddin). A former judge (kadıasker) in Musa Çelebi's administration, Bedreddin was an influential theologian with a growing following. After Musa's defeat, Bedreddin retreated to the Balkans, where he began advocating for a more egalitarian and communal form of society that resonated with peasants and disenfranchised groups.

By 1416–1417, Bedreddin's movement had turned into open revolt, with pockets of support in both Rumelia and Anatolia. Mehmed moved decisively against this challenge, deploying loyal governors to suppress the rebels. Bedreddin was eventually captured and executed, but his teachings continued to influence certain heterodox communities in the empire for centuries. The swift crackdown illustrated Mehmed's determination to maintain centralized control and avoid further fragmentation.

The Karamanid Threat

Meanwhile, in central Anatolia, the Karamanid Beylik posed perennial threats to Ottoman stability. Although Mehmed had subdued them diplomatically, periodic skirmishes and border disputes continued. Mehmed balanced aggression with treaty-making, ensuring the Karamanids could never rally a large coalition against him. This tension would continue under subsequent sultans, reflecting the deep-rooted rivalries that persisted among the Turkish principalities long after the Interregnum.

9. MEHMED I'S FOREIGN RELATIONS

Relations with the Byzantine Empire

Having benefited from Byzantine support during the Interregnum (and vice versa), Mehmed I maintained a guarded peace with Constantinople. While he did not abandon Ottoman ambitions regarding the city, he recognized that immediate conquest was neither feasible nor prudent. Thus, he concluded temporary treaties, ensuring that trade between Thrace and Constantinople continued and that the Byzantines would not sponsor new pretenders to the Ottoman throne.

Balkan Principalities

In the Balkans, Mehmed recognized that stability was crucial for rebuilding the empire's war-ravaged economy. He renewed vassal treaties with Serbia and Wallachia, allowing local rulers to maintain authority in exchange for tribute and military support. Bosnia, under the control of local nobility and sometimes influenced by Hungary, also navigated a delicate relationship with Mehmed's court. By avoiding overly harsh demands, Mehmed reduced the likelihood of broad coalitions forming against him.

Western Powers

Venice and Genoa, the major maritime republics, sought trading privileges in the newly re-stabilized Ottoman lands. Mehmed, eager to boost revenues, granted capitulations (special economic rights) to these Italian powers, fostering commerce in port cities along the Aegean and the Sea of Marmara. This flow of goods and merchants also helped in the empire's reconstruction efforts.

10. CULTURAL AND ADMINISTRATIVE REVIVAL

Patronage of Learning and Arts

Though overshadowed in later centuries by sultans like Mehmed II and Suleiman the Magnificent, Mehmed I did encourage the arts and scholarship to a degree.

Poets and religious scholars found patronage at his court. In cities such as Bursa and Edirne, new madrasas were established or old ones restored, reflecting a revival of educational institutions after the disruptions of the Interregnum.

Restoration of Architecture

Mehmed also focused on architectural endeavors to signal a return to normalcy. Mosques destroyed during the civil war were rebuilt, caravanserais were repaired, and markets reopened. Such visible improvements helped reassure the populace that the Ottoman state had overcome its internal strife and was once again on a path of prosperity.

11. THE FINAL YEARS OF MEHMED I

Emergence of a Resilient Empire

By the 1420s, Mehmed I had managed to reforge the Ottoman Empire into a coherent state. Although not as large or consolidated as it had been before Ankara, the empire was once again a formidable power, controlling vital trade routes and possessing a loyal core army. The administration, now more experienced in crisis management, was better prepared to face future challenges.

Succession Planning

Mehmed I had seen first-hand the devastation wrought by an unclear line of succession. Determined to avoid a repeat of the Interregnum, he worked to smooth the path for his son Murad, ensuring the young prince had both governorship experience and the loyalty of key military commanders and viziers. By the time Mehmed died in 1421, the empire was in a much stronger position than it had been at the start of his reign.

12. CONCLUSION OF CHAPTER 5

Mehmed I's story is one of resilience. In the aftermath of the empire's near-collapse, his steady leadership restored unity. He subdued rival siblings, quelled rebellions like that of Sheikh Bedreddin, managed the complexities of Balkan and Anatolian politics, and maintained a careful balance with the Byzantine Empire and other foreign powers.

The Interregnum tested the empire's limits. It exposed vulnerabilities in the Ottoman succession system and in the balance of power between the central government and outlying regions. Still, under Mehmed's watchful eye, those weaknesses were gradually addressed. By the time of his death, the Ottomans had survived what could have been a fatal blow. They were now poised once again for expansion and consolidation, setting the stage for the reign of Murad II.

CHAPTER 6

THE AGE OF MURAD II

Succeeding Mehmed I in 1421, Murad II inherited an empire that had just overcome the tumult of the Interregnum. While much of the realm had been consolidated, challenges remained. Regional powers in the Balkans were restless, various Anatolian beyliks tested Ottoman resolve, and the Byzantine Empire still held onto Constantinople. Murad's reign would prove both dynamic and tumultuous, spanning nearly three decades that included internal revolts, significant battles with Christian coalitions, and notable diplomatic achievements. Crucially, Murad II also set the stage for his successor—Mehmed II—who would eventually capture Constantinople.

1. ACCESSION CRISIS AND EARLY CHALLENGES

Murad's Ascension to Power

Mehmed I's careful grooming of Murad minimized immediate succession strife. Nevertheless, upon Mehmed's death in 1421, some factions were quick to question Murad's authority. Rival claimants—real or invented—appeared, claiming descent from Bayezid I. The Byzantine Emperor, John VIII Palaiologos (acting alongside his father Manuel II), saw an opportunity to sow discord among the Ottomans and supported one such pretender, named **Mustafa Çelebi** (often called "Düzmece Mustafa," meaning "Fake Mustafa").

Murad, still a young ruler, swiftly consolidated support within the Ottoman military and bureaucracy, but the emergence of Mustafa forced Murad to divide his attention between the Balkans and Anatolia. In addition, some smaller beyliks in central Anatolia tested the new sultan's mettle by refusing tribute or harboring rebels.

Mustafa's Rebellion

Supported by Byzantine ships, Mustafa crossed from the Byzantine-controlled territories into Rumelia, rallying local notables who were disappointed or resentful following Mehmed I's rule. Initially, he gained traction, capturing some strongholds. However, Murad sent a seasoned army under trusted commanders to confront Mustafa. In the end, the pretender was betrayed by local allies who recognized Murad's growing advantage. Mustafa was captured and executed, ending the immediate threat.

2. RELATIONS WITH THE BYZANTINE EMPIRE

Siege of Constantinople (1422)

Outraged by the Byzantines' support of Mustafa, Murad decided to strike at the heart of their power: Constantinople. By laying siege to the city, he aimed not only to punish Emperor John VIII but also to assert Ottoman dominance. The siege, launched in 1422, involved heavy artillery bombardment—a precursor to the larger-scale siege that would come later under Mehmed II.

Despite intense pressure, Constantinople withstood the assault. The city's formidable walls, along with the defenders' desperate resolve, forced Murad to lift the siege. Internal concerns in Anatolia (a rebellion in Bursa) also diverted his attention, compelling him to withdraw. Although the siege ended in failure, it set a precedent for future Ottoman campaigns against Constantinople.

Diplomatic Maneuvers

Following the failed siege, Murad recognized that conquering Constantinople would be no easy task. He shifted to a strategy of diplomatic pressure and containment. The Byzantines, for their part, were eager to keep the Ottomans off-balance by supporting or at least threatening to support rival claimants to the Ottoman throne. Through a combination of tribute demands, short-term truces, and occasional blockades of the Bosporus, Murad kept the empire's grip on the city's hinterlands strong.

3. ANATOLIAN CAMPAIGNS AND REBELLIONS

Revolt in Bursa (1422)

Even as he besieged Constantinople, Murad learned of a rebellion in Bursa led by another pretender, sometimes identified as **Küçük Mustafa** (another "Mustafa"). This revolt, supported by disgruntled military officers and local elites, posed a direct threat to Murad's authority in the old Ottoman capital. Murad ended the Constantinople siege prematurely to deal with this crisis. He marched back to Anatolia, subdued the rebels, and ensured Bursa's loyalty through swift punitive measures.

Karamanid Conflict

The Karamanid Beylik, centered in Konya, remained a perennial thorn in the Ottomans' side. During the Interregnum, the Karamanids had regained independence and territory. Murad II, determined to reassert Ottoman authority, launched multiple campaigns into Karamanid lands. While some battles were decisive, the Karamanids proved resilient, often retreating into the Taurus Mountains or striking Ottoman lines of communication.

To manage this ongoing conflict, Murad sometimes engaged in marriage diplomacy—offering or receiving noblewomen to solidify peace agreements. At other times, he used brute force, capturing Karamanid strongholds and installing Ottoman-friendly governors.

The Germiyanids and Other Beyliks

Beyond the Karamanids, other beyliks such as Germiyan, Aydın, and Menteşe demanded attention. Many of these beyliks had sworn loyalty to Mehmed I, yet remained opportunistic. Murad navigated these relationships carefully, rewarding loyal beys with titles and land grants, while swiftly punishing any sign of rebellion. Gradually, the tapestry of Anatolian beyliks was drawn ever tighter into the Ottoman sphere, though the process was neither smooth nor swift.

4. MILITARY REFORMS AND ADMINISTRATION UNDER MURAD II

Janissaries and Provincial Armies

Building on his father's foundation, Murad expanded the Janissary corps, ensuring this elite infantry had better training, equipment, and pay. He also enhanced the provincial timar system for cavalry, granting lands to loyal sipahis who provided mounted troops in wartime. The balancing act between Janissaries (central authority) and sipahi cavalry (local authority) would remain a hallmark of Ottoman military organization for centuries.

To bolster the empire's finances, Murad revisited tax structures, ensuring the treasury could support a standing army even during peacetime. He also encouraged the growth of crafts and trade within Ottoman cities, aiming to generate revenue through market taxes and customs duties.

Civil Administration

Murad appointed experienced administrators to high office, many of whom had served under Mehmed I. The viziers and kadıaskers played critical roles in streamlining legal codes and ensuring law and order across the empire's diverse population. Under Murad, the Ottoman bureaucracy became more standardized, with clearer hierarchies and more formal record-keeping (defter). This increased administrative efficiency, helping to prevent corruption and bolster the sultan's control.

5. BALKAN STRATEGY: DIPLOMACY AND WAR

Shifting Alliances

In the Balkans, Murad faced a complex landscape of Christian states—Hungary, Serbia, Bosnia, Wallachia—alongside various principalities and local lords. The Ottomans already had enclaves of territory in Thrace, Macedonia, and Bulgaria. Some Balkan rulers, like Serbian Despot George Branković, alternately allied with or rebelled against the Ottomans, depending on immediate self-interest.

Murad used a mixture of armed force and diplomatic treaties to maintain Ottoman influence. He allowed certain vassal states to retain their ruling dynasties as long as they paid tribute and supplied troops when called upon. In times of rebellion, or if a local ruler sought external help (e.g., from Hungary),

Murad responded with swift military campaigns, capturing key fortresses and reaffirming his overlordship.

The Role of Hungary

Hungary emerged as the principal antagonist in the Balkans. Kings Sigismund and, later, Albert II maintained alliances with other Balkan states, fearing further Ottoman expansion. Though large-scale crusades were less frequent after Nicopolis (1396), cross-border raids and limited conflicts became a recurrent pattern. Each side tested the other's defenses, capturing outposts or conducting punitive forays.

6. THE CRUSADES OF VARNA AND THE LONG CAMPAIGN

Background to the Crusade

European fears of Ottoman expansion did not vanish after the Interregnum. In the 1440s, Pope Eugenius IV and other leaders renewed calls for a crusade, spurred by King Władysław III of Poland (who was also King of Hungary) and John Hunyadi, the regent-governor of Hungary. They aimed to push the Ottomans out of the Balkans altogether and, ideally, reclaim Constantinople for Christendom.

A series of military campaigns—often referred to as the **Long Campaign**—took shape around 1443. Hunyadi led Hungarian and Polish forces deep into Ottoman territory. Initially, they achieved some success, exploiting winter conditions that confounded the Ottoman defenders. Murad II's forces retreated, reorganizing over the harsh season.

Murad's Abdication and Return

In a surprising twist, Murad abdicated briefly in 1444 in favor of his young son, Mehmed II, possibly due to personal exhaustion or to domestic political pressures. He retreated to Manisa in western Anatolia, intending to live a quieter life. However, the timing was unfortunate: as soon as word of his abdication spread, the European crusader forces saw an opportunity. When they launched a renewed offensive, the inexperienced Mehmed II struggled to manage the crisis. In desperation, the Ottoman leadership and Mehmed's own advisors appealed to Murad to return to the throne.

Reassuming power, Murad led the Ottoman army to confront the crusaders near the Black Sea port city of Varna in 1444. The **Battle of Varna** proved decisive. Murad's forces overwhelmed the crusaders; King Władysław III was killed in the fighting, and Hunyadi retreated. This victory effectively ended the immediate threat of a large-scale Balkan crusade.

Significance of Varna

The Battle of Varna solidified Ottoman control in the lower Danube region. It also reaffirmed Murad's stature as a capable sultan. His return to power underscored that stable leadership was essential to repelling coordinated European attacks. Varna became one of the defining battles of Murad's reign, a moment that convinced many Balkan states that direct confrontation with the Ottomans was unwise.

7. SECOND ABDICATION AND REASSUMPTION OF POWER

Political Maneuvers

Despite the victory at Varna, Murad attempted another retirement a few years later. The exact motives remain debated among historians. Some suggest he yearned for a more pious life away from constant warfare; others argue he sought to test the empire's readiness under Mehmed's leadership. This second abdication, however, led once more to instability.

In 1446, the Janissaries in Edirne revolted, dissatisfied with Mehmed's policies and lacking confidence in the teenage sultan's rule. The revolt, called the **Buca Incident** by some chroniclers, forced Mehmed to request Murad's return again. Murad took the throne once more, securing the loyalty of the Janissaries by increasing their pay and reaffirming their privileged status.

Battle of the Second Kosovo (1448)

Shortly after Murad's second restoration, John Hunyadi led another crusading force, hoping to avenge Varna's defeat. The two sides met at the **Second Battle of Kosovo** in 1448. The Ottomans again prevailed. Hunyadi's forces, though sizable, lacked the cohesive support of all European powers, and Ottoman tactics—combined with local Balkan vassal support—secured the victory. This second battle of Kosovo cemented Ottoman authority in the region for decades. With no major Balkan coalition left to challenge them effectively, the Ottomans enjoyed a relatively stable frontier.

8. INTERNAL GOVERNANCE AND SOCIAL POLICIES UNDER MURAD II

Court Culture

Murad II's court was known for its patronage of literature and music. He was personally interested in poetry, and some accounts credit him with encouraging a cultural renaissance in Edirne. Prominent scholars, poets, and artists found refuge under his rule, contributing to a sophisticated courtly environment. Although overshadowed in later centuries by the cultural achievements of Suleiman the Magnificent, Murad's reign laid important groundwork, particularly in encouraging Ottoman language and poetic forms.

Construction and Public Works

Murad II invested in architectural projects, especially in Edirne. He built mosques, bridges, and caravanserais to facilitate trade and demonstrate the sultan's benevolence. Among his notable contributions is the **Muradiye Mosque** complex, which included a soup kitchen (imaret) and other charitable facilities. These public works helped unify the empire's diverse populations, showcasing the sultan's role as both warrior and patron of civic life.

9. LEGACY OF MURAD II

By the time of his death in 1451, Murad II had experienced more than his share of warfare, abdications, and reconquests. Yet, he left the empire in a markedly stronger position than he found it:

1. **Stabilized Succession**: Murad's repeated abdications were unorthodox, but they allowed Mehmed II to gain valuable experience in governance before eventually becoming sultan in his own right—this time without interference.
2. **Balkan Dominance**: Victories at Varna (1444) and the Second Kosovo (1448) ensured the Ottomans remained the dominant power in southeastern Europe. Although future conflicts would arise, no major crusading effort threatened the empire for some time.
3. **Continued Centralization**: Murad's expansion of the Janissary corps and refinement of the Ottoman bureaucracy furthered the centralization efforts initiated by his predecessors. This strengthened the empire's core structures.
4. **Cultural Flourishing**: Through support of the arts, poetry, and architecture, Murad's court at Edirne helped solidify a distinctly Ottoman cultural identity.

Nevertheless, certain challenges lingered. The Byzantine Empire, though diminished, still held Constantinople—a potent symbol of imperial ambition for the Ottomans. The Karamanids in Anatolia remained defiant. And though the Balkans were largely subdued, discontent simmered among local Christian populations.

CHAPTER 7

THE CONQUEST OF CONSTANTINOPLE BY MEHMED II

With the death of Murad II in 1451, the Ottoman throne passed for the second time to his son **Mehmed II**. Although still quite young—likely around 19 years old—Mehmed had already experienced governance during his father's brief abdications. Now, with the full weight of the empire on his shoulders, he was determined to achieve a momentous goal that had eluded previous sultans: the capture of Constantinople. This chapter explores Mehmed II's preparations for the siege, the decisive military innovations he employed, the dramatic fall of the Byzantine capital in May 1453, and the immediate transformations that followed.

1. MEHMED II'S EARLY PREPARATIONS

Securing the Throne and Empire

Following Murad II's death, Mehmed II quickly consolidated power. He reassured key military officers and administrators of their positions, ensuring loyalty within the army and bureaucracy. He also addressed any lingering opposition. By this time, the empire was relatively stable compared to the tumultuous periods of the past. The Balkans, while not free of unrest, posed fewer immediate threats since recent Ottoman victories had discouraged large-scale coalitions.

Within Anatolia, most major beyliks had been subdued or were content under Ottoman suzerainty. Mehmed's primary focus was thus turned toward Byzantium, whose once-great empire was reduced to the city of Constantinople and a few outlying territories. Still, Constantinople's symbolic and strategic importance remained immense.

The Strategic Importance of Constantinople

Constantinople was uniquely located, straddling the narrow Bosporus Strait between Europe and Asia. Controlling this city would grant the Ottomans a powerful bridgehead linking their Balkan and Anatolian possessions. Moreover, Constantinople was a major hub for regional trade, connecting the Black Sea to the Mediterranean. For Mehmed, capturing this historic metropolis was not only a matter of prestige but also a practical step to unify and enrich the Ottoman realm.

Even beyond economics and geography, Constantinople carried religious and cultural significance. It was the seat of the Eastern Orthodox Church and a city of ancient Roman and Byzantine emperors. Since the city's founding by Emperor Constantine in 330, many had called it "The Queen of Cities." Mehmed saw himself as the rightful heir to that legacy, a conqueror destined to take the capital that had withstood numerous sieges for over a millennium.

---

2. BUILDING RUMELI HISARI AND PREPARING FOR SIEGE

Fortifying the Bosporus

One of Mehmed's first major steps was constructing a fortress on the European side of the Bosporus—**Rumeli Hisarı**—directly opposite the earlier Ottoman fortress of Anadolu Hisarı on the Asian side. Begun in 1452, this massive project was completed in a matter of months. Its purpose was straightforward: to control naval traffic through the Bosporus and cut off Constantinople from any Black Sea aid.

With heavy artillery placements in Rumeli Hisarı, any ship attempting to resupply the Byzantine capital risked being sunk. This blockade was essential to Mehmed's strategy. He wanted to isolate Constantinople, preventing supplies and reinforcements from reaching Emperor Constantine XI Palaiologos.

Diplomatic Maneuvers

As the fortress rose, diplomatic tensions spiked. The Byzantine Emperor and European powers saw Rumeli Hisarı for what it was—an unmistakable sign that the Ottomans planned a full-scale attack on Constantinople. Some Latin states, including Venice and Genoa, contemplated supporting the Byzantine defenders, but their response was hesitant and fragmented. Mehmed skillfully balanced shows of force with reassurances to nearby European states, suggesting he had no quarrel with them as long as they did not interfere.

In parallel, Mehmed made sure to maintain relatively peaceful conditions with Hungary and other potential foes, so no coordinated Christian coalition would form prematurely. He offered temporary truces or renewed tribute agreements with regional princes, ensuring the Ottoman focus could remain solely on Constantinople.

3. OTTOMAN ARTILLERY INNOVATIONS

The Foundry and the Master Gunner

One of the decisive factors in the siege was the **heavy artillery** produced under Mehmed's direction. He recruited skilled cannon-makers, notably the Hungarian engineer **Urban** (or Orban), who had previously offered his services to the Byzantine court but was turned away due to lack of funds.

Urban's expertise, combined with Ottoman resources, led to the casting of massive bombard cannons. These guns could fire large stone or metal projectiles at formidable ranges. While the technology of gunpowder weaponry was still evolving, Mehmed's emphasis on large-scale artillery gave the Ottomans a significant edge.

Types of Cannons

In addition to the mammoth bombard, the Ottoman siege train included smaller culverins, falcons, and mortars. Such diversity allowed Ottoman forces to pound the city walls continuously, targeting different heights and thicknesses. Though these early cannons were cumbersome and prone to misfires, their psychological impact was immense. The thunderous blasts demoralized defenders and inflicted real damage to the ancient fortifications.

4. THE STATE OF BYZANTINE DEFENSES

Byzantine Defensive Preparations

Constantine XI and his advisors knew a siege was imminent. The city's population had dwindled over the centuries, and its defensive perimeter was large relative to available manpower. However, the famous **Theodosian Walls** were still robust, consisting of multiple layers: a deep moat, outer wall, and the towering inner wall. While formidable, these walls had not been thoroughly modernized to withstand prolonged cannon bombardments.

In desperation, Constantine XI sought aid from Catholic Europe, but religious schisms between Catholic and Orthodox Christians hampered a united front. A small contingent of Genoese and Venetian mercenaries did arrive, bringing valuable expertise, but the total number of defenders was still inadequate. Estimates suggest the city had between 5,000 and 7,000 defenders—both Byzantines and foreign allies—against an Ottoman army possibly exceeding 50,000 to 80,000 or more.

Strengthening the Chain Boom

A crucial defensive measure was the **chain boom** that stretched across the Golden Horn, preventing Ottoman ships from easily entering the city's harbor. This chain was anchored at the Tower of Eugenius on the city side and Galata (a Genoese district) on the other. Byzantine and allied vessels positioned behind the boom offered some naval protection.

Yet this naval defense was not invulnerable. The Ottomans had started constructing a fleet on the Sea of Marmara, intending to cut off all seaward escape routes. Moreover, Mehmed had a plan for circumventing the chain that would become legendary during the siege.

5. THE SIEGE BEGINS (APRIL 1453)

Initial Bombardment

By early April 1453, Ottoman troops encircled Constantinople. Mehmed established his main camp on the northwestern side, near the Lycus River valley, a weak point in the city walls. Once in position, the great bombard commenced firing, sending shockwaves through the Byzantine defenses. Though rate of fire was slow (sometimes just a few shots per day due to barrel overheating and the need for repositioning), the psychological effect was immense.

Simultaneously, smaller Ottoman guns fired more frequently, attempting to chip away at the outer walls. Sappers dug tunnels to undermine the fortifications, though Byzantine counter-tunnels thwarted many efforts. Skirmishes broke out near the moat as Ottoman troops tested the city's response.

Naval Blockade and the Golden Horn

The Ottoman fleet patrolled the Sea of Marmara, preventing Byzantine reinforcements or supplies from the south. A small number of Byzantine and allied vessels remained behind the chain boom in the Golden Horn, where the

Ottomans could not easily reach them. Mehmed attempted several naval assaults but was initially repelled by well-positioned defenders on the walls.

A critical setback came on April 20, when a handful of Genoese ships managed to slip past the Ottoman blockade with food and reinforcements. This success boosted the defenders' morale. Mehmed, furious at his navy's failure, reorganized his admirals and resolved to tighten the sea blockade further.

6. THE TRANSPORT OF OTTOMAN SHIPS OVER LAND

Innovative Tactic

Frustrated by the stalemate at the chain in the Golden Horn, Mehmed devised a bold plan. He ordered the construction of a **wooden slipway** across the Galata hills, greased with animal fat. Under cover of darkness, Ottoman soldiers and laborers hauled dozens of ships out of the Bosporus, dragging them over land into the Golden Horn above the chain. By the morning, the defenders awoke to find a fleet of Ottoman galleys positioned inside what they had believed was their secure harbor.

This maneuver is often regarded as one of the most ingenious feats of the siege. It effectively nullified the chain boom and exposed the city's sea-facing walls to direct naval attacks.

Impact on Morale

For the defenders, seeing Ottoman ships within the Golden Horn was a devastating blow. They now faced bombardments on multiple fronts and lost control of crucial waterfront areas. Though they fought bravely, the Byzantines were stretched thin. Emperor Constantine XI tried to fortify the harbor walls, but the sudden shift in naval superiority gave Mehmed a decisive advantage.

7. FINAL ASSAULT: MAY 1453

Widening the Breaches

Through late April and early May, Ottoman artillery pounded sections of the Theodosian Walls relentlessly. The greatest damage was inflicted near the **Gate of St. Romanus** (Topkapı area), where repeated bombardments caused large breaches. Ottoman infantry probes tested these gaps, but the defenders, led by famed Genoese commander **Giovanni Giustiniani**, managed to hold off each assault.

On May 29, Mehmed ordered an all-out offensive. He divided his army into waves. The first wave consisted of irregular troops (bashi-bazouks), tasked with wearing down the defenders and exhausting their resources. The second wave, formed of Anatolian troops, followed closely. Finally, Mehmed's elite Janissaries advanced, focusing on the weakened gate defenses.

The Fall of the City

Despite fierce resistance, the defenders were overwhelmed. Giustiniani was severely wounded, causing a collapse in the Byzantine morale on that section of the wall. Ottoman flags were soon raised on the ramparts. Emperor Constantine XI reportedly died in the fighting, choosing to go down with his city rather than flee.

By midday on May 29, 1453, Ottoman soldiers had entered Constantinople. They secured key gates, overpowered remaining pockets of resistance, and claimed the city in Mehmed's name. After more than a thousand years as the Byzantine capital, Constantinople had fallen to the Ottomans.

8. THE AFTERMATH AND MEHMED'S ENTRY

A Triumphant Arrival

Later that day, Mehmed II made a ceremonial entry into the city. Though some looting occurred in the initial chaos, Mehmed quickly put a stop to it, recognizing the city's potential value if preserved. He rode through the battered streets, marveling at Constantinople's grand churches and palaces. His first stop was the **Hagia Sophia**, the great cathedral of the city, which he ordered to be protected. Soon after, Hagia Sophia would be converted into a mosque—a potent symbol of the city's transformation under Ottoman rule.

Mehmed allowed Greek Orthodox Christians to remain, appointing a new Patriarch to oversee the community. This pragmatic approach helped ensure stability in a city whose population was now largely non-Muslim. Over time, the sultan encouraged resettlement by attracting Muslims, Christians, and Jews from other parts of the empire, revitalizing the depopulated metropolis.

Renaming and Rebuilding

Mehmed declared Constantinople to be the new Ottoman capital. Though the official Ottoman name would evolve, eventually becoming **"Istanbul,"** the city's reinvention had begun immediately. In the months that followed, the sultan commissioned repairs to the walls, construction of new buildings, and the establishment of markets and districts for artisans. His aim was to restore the city's position as a major commercial and cultural center.

9. INTERNATIONAL REACTION

Shock in Europe

The fall of Constantinople sent shockwaves through Christian Europe. Centuries of unsuccessful Muslim attempts to seize the city had shaped a widespread belief in its invincibility. Now, with the city in Ottoman hands, merchants, diplomats, and kings alike scrambled to reassess their strategies. Some Italian city-states worried about their trade routes in the eastern Mediterranean, while others feared the Ottomans might use Constantinople as a springboard for further expansion into Europe.

Eastern Muslim Views

In the Muslim world, Mehmed's victory was celebrated. Poets hailed him as the **"new Alexander"** and the "Conqueror of the Two Continents." His prestige soared across Anatolia, the Middle East, and beyond. Cities like Cairo and Damascus recognized that the Ottomans had become the leading Sunni power in the region. Eventually, this rising Ottoman influence would shift the balance of power in the Islamic world, particularly with the empire's later control over the holy cities of Mecca and Medina under Selim I.

10. LEGACY AND SIGNIFICANCE OF 1453

End of the Byzantine Empire

The conquest of Constantinople effectively ended the Byzantine Empire, which had been a central player in Mediterranean and European politics for over a millennium. Although a few Byzantine successor states, like the Empire of Trebizond, lingered for a short time, none challenged the Ottomans' dominance. For historians, the fall of Constantinople often marks the end of the medieval era and the start of early modern history in southeastern Europe.

Mehmed II's Emerging Vision

With his triumph in Constantinople, Mehmed II earned the epithet **"Fatih,"** or "the Conqueror." He was only in his early twenties, but his ambition was boundless. In capturing this legendary city, he demonstrated political acumen, military innovation, and willingness to adopt foreign technology. The conquest paved the way for even more radical reforms, as Mehmed sought to remake the Ottoman Empire into a central authority ruling over a diverse, cosmopolitan population.

CHAPTER 8

MEHMED II'S REFORMS AND CONQUESTS AFTER 1453

In the wake of Constantinople's fall, **Mehmed II "the Conqueror"** set about restructuring the empire to match his ambitious vision. He transformed Constantinople (soon to be known as Istanbul) into a vibrant capital, introduced sweeping administrative reforms, and pressed forward with new conquests in Europe and Asia. This chapter traces Mehmed's post-1453 initiatives, including his centralizing policies, cultural patronage, and major military campaigns until his death in 1481. By laying robust institutional foundations, Mehmed arguably shaped the Ottoman Empire for centuries to come.

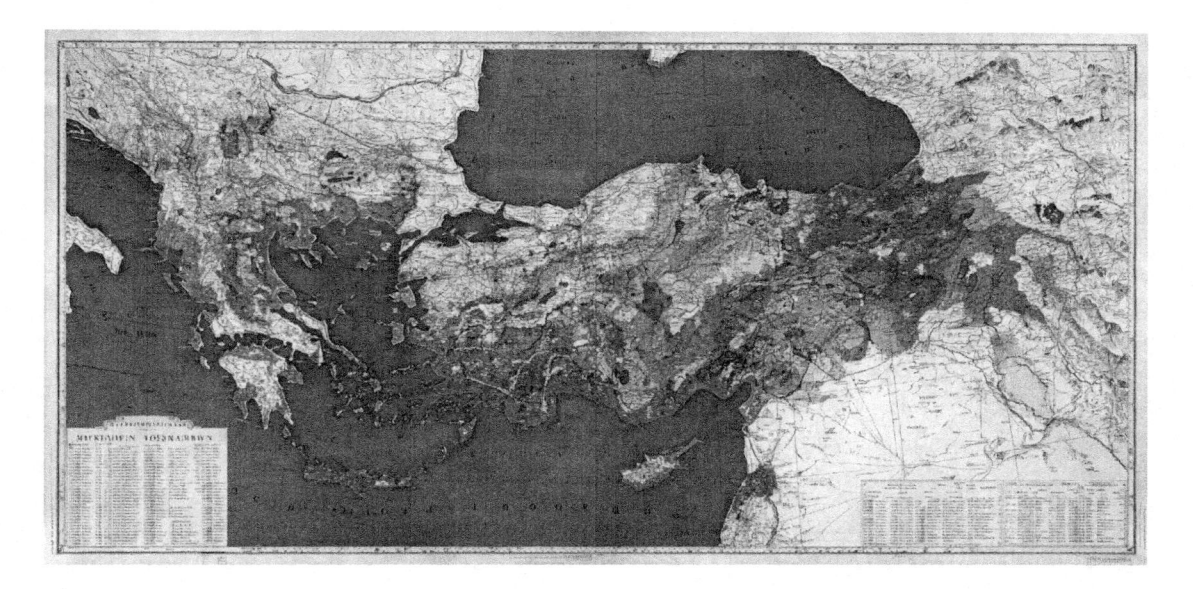

1. REBUILDING AND REPOPULATING CONSTANTINOPLE

Urban Planning Efforts

When Mehmed entered Constantinople, he found a city significantly reduced by centuries of warfare, plagues, and declining trade. Large swaths of land inside the walls were overgrown or in ruins. Determined to restore its grandeur, Mehmed encouraged people from various parts of the empire—Muslims, Christians, Jews—to settle in the city. He offered tax incentives, gave out vacant homes, and rebuilt essential infrastructure such as aqueducts and markets.

Key projects included:

- **Repairing the Theodosian Walls** to ensure the capital remained defensible.
- **Revitalizing the Grand Bazaar** area, turning it into a thriving commercial hub.
- **Constructing new mosques**, including the first imperial complex (Fatih Mosque) on the site of the old Church of the Holy Apostles.

Multicultural Character

Mehmed wanted Istanbul to be a cosmopolitan center. He allowed the Greek Orthodox community to maintain its patriarch under Ottoman supervision, thus minimizing religious tensions. He also recognized the Armenian Patriarchate and welcomed Jewish communities fleeing persecution in other parts of Europe. Over time, Istanbul became an ethnically and religiously diverse metropolis that reflected the empire's broader policy of pragmatic tolerance—so long as subjects paid taxes and accepted Ottoman sovereignty.

2. ADMINISTRATIVE REFORMS AND CENTRALIZATION

The Kanun and Legal Codification

One of Mehmed's most lasting contributions was the establishment of a more systematic legal code, often referred to collectively as **Kanun** (secular law). While

Islamic Sharia remained foundational for personal and religious matters, Mehmed recognized the need for additional regulations covering taxation, property rights, and governance. Drawing upon past Seljuk, Byzantine, and local Anatolian precedents, Mehmed's Kanun aimed to standardize administrative practices across diverse regions.

He also reorganized the **Divan**, the imperial council of viziers and high officials. Previously, the sultan often presided directly over these meetings. Mehmed sometimes delegated this role to his **Grand Vizier**, freeing himself for larger strategic concerns. This shift marked a step toward a more modern bureaucratic state, in which professional administrators carried out daily governance.

Succession Policies

The Interregnum's chaos had taught the Ottomans the dangers of unclear succession. Mehmed introduced practices that, while harsh, sought to prevent civil wars between siblings. He issued edicts allowing a new sultan to eliminate potential rivals among his brothers to secure undisputed rule. Over time, this policy evolved into the infamous practice of fratricide. Though brutal, it was justified by many Ottoman rulers as necessary to preserve state stability.

3. THE IMPERIAL PALACE AND COURT CULTURE

Topkapı Palace

To symbolize the empire's new imperial identity, Mehmed II commissioned the construction of **Topkapı Palace** on the site of the old Byzantine acropolis, overlooking the Bosporus. This sprawling complex replaced the smaller palaces used by previous sultans. It served as both the administrative center and the sultan's residence. Over the following centuries, Topkapı Palace expanded into a city within a city—housing the harem, treasury, council chambers, gardens, and pavilions.

Patronage of Arts and Learning

Mehmed was an enthusiastic patron of the arts. He invited scholars, poets, and artisans from across the Islamic world and Europe. He sponsored translations of Greek and Latin texts into Turkish and Arabic, encouraging a cultural exchange that enriched Ottoman intellectual life. Italian Renaissance influence also seeped in, as Mehmed admired Western art and even employed Italian artists like Gentile Bellini for portraiture.

4. CONSOLIDATING POWER IN THE BALKANS

Wars in Serbia and Bosnia

After seizing Constantinople, Mehmed turned his attention to consolidating Ottoman rule in the Balkans. Serbia, under Despot George Branković, still maintained partial independence. Mehmed launched campaigns to bring Serbian lands fully under Ottoman control. By 1459, the Ottomans captured **Smederevo**, the last major Serbian stronghold, effectively ending the medieval Serbian Despotate.

Bosnia was another priority. The Ottomans had long exercised influence there, but local feudal lords occasionally rebelled. Mehmed's forces captured **Bobovac** and key fortresses, cementing Ottoman authority. Some Bosnian nobles converted to Islam to retain land and status under Ottoman overlordship, reflecting the sultan's ability to integrate conquered elites into his administration.

Conflict with Hungary

Hungary continued to pose a threat, particularly under the leadership of John Hunyadi's successors and, later, King Matthias Corvinus. Mehmed sought to secure borders along the Danube, fortifying key river towns and forging alliances with Wallachian princes who also guarded their autonomy. While major battles like Varna (1444) had already shaped Ottoman-Hungarian relations, skirmishes and short-term truces remained a recurring pattern throughout Mehmed's reign. Neither side could fully subdue the other, leading to a tense but largely stable frontier.

5. CAMPAIGNS IN THE AEGEAN AND BLACK SEA

The Morea and the Despotate

The **Morea** (the Peloponnese peninsula in southern Greece) was partly ruled by remnants of the Byzantine Palaiologos family. In the aftermath of 1453, the Despots of the Morea tried to garner Western support against the Ottomans. Mehmed launched multiple expeditions into the region, capturing important strongholds like **Mistra**. By the early 1460s, the Ottomans had overrun the Morea, removing one of the last Byzantine successor states.

The Empire of Trebizond

Another Byzantine successor state was the **Empire of Trebizond** on the Black Sea coast, centered in modern-day Trabzon. Trebizond was rich due to Black Sea trade, though geographically isolated. Mehmed demanded tribute, and when Trebizond resisted, he led a campaign in 1461 that ended in its surrender. This marked the final extinguishing of Byzantine imperial lineage. With Trebizond under Ottoman control, the Black Sea became increasingly an Ottoman "lake," dominated by their fleets and coastal garrisons.

Relations with Venice and Genoa

Venice and Genoa held numerous coastal colonies and islands in the Aegean and Black Sea. Conflicts arose over trade rights and territorial claims. Mehmed recognized the economic benefits of allowing Italians to maintain commercial operations in Ottoman ports, but he also aimed to limit their political influence. Periodic wars with Venice flared, most notably over islands like **Euboea (Negroponte)**, which the Ottomans eventually seized. Despite these hostilities, trade often continued, with Venetian and Genoese merchants paying taxes to operate in Ottoman markets.

6. EASTERN EXPANSIONS AND DIPLOMACY

Moves Against the Karamanids

In central Anatolia, the Karamanid Beylik remained a persistent issue. Under Mehmed II, the Ottomans launched several campaigns to finally subdue Karaman. By capturing Konya and Karamanid fortresses, Mehmed extended firm control over much of central Anatolia. Though pockets of resistance lingered, the Karamanids were reduced to a minor presence. This consolidation further strengthened Ottoman unity in Anatolia.

Contact with the Mamluks

To the south, the Mamluk Sultanate in Egypt and Syria was a major Islamic power. Mehmed carefully managed relations, as open warfare against the Mamluks could drain Ottoman resources and hamper pilgrimage routes to Mecca and Medina. While border disputes and occasional skirmishes occurred near southeastern Anatolia, Mehmed mostly maintained peace with the Mamluks, focusing instead on European expansions. It would fall to later sultans, like Selim I, to alter this balance drastically.

7. INTERNAL POLICIES AND THE DEVŞIRME SYSTEM

Expansion of the Janissaries

Mehmed II further developed the **devşirme** (child levy) system, in which Christian youths from the Balkans were taken, converted to Islam, and trained for military or administrative service. This practice allowed Mehmed to maintain a loyal and skilled cadre of soldiers known as the Janissaries. Though the system had begun earlier, Mehmed expanded it, seeing the Janissaries as a crucial instrument of central authority.

The Janissaries enjoyed special privileges, including regular salaries and direct allegiance to the sultan, thus strengthening the throne. Over time, they became a powerful military elite that played a significant role in Ottoman politics.

Timar System Revisions

Mehmed also refined the **timar** system, whereby cavalry soldiers (sipahis) received land grants in exchange for military service. He introduced stricter record-keeping to prevent abuses and ensure that each timar holder was accountable for supplying troops. These measures helped stabilize provincial governance, tying local interests to the sultan's success.

By centralizing power in Istanbul and ensuring administrative loyalty, Mehmed reduced the autonomy of provincial notables who could otherwise challenge the throne. This created a more cohesive state apparatus, though it also meant the empire was increasingly governed by officials appointed from the capital rather than by local dynasties.

8. CULTURAL INTEGRATION AND RELIGIOUS DIVERSITY

Patronage of Religion

Although Mehmed embraced Islam as the empire's guiding faith, he maintained the **millet** system that allowed non-Muslim communities to govern many of their own affairs under Ottoman oversight. This approach drew upon earlier precedents of religious toleration, ensuring that Orthodox Christians, Armenians, and Jews could practice their faiths relatively freely. Leaders of these communities—such as the Greek Orthodox Patriarch—were granted official status and became intermediaries between their flocks and the Ottoman authorities.

Language and Scholarship

The Ottoman court language shifted toward a refined form of Turkish heavily influenced by Persian and Arabic. Mehmed supported translations of classic works from Greek, Persian, and Arabic into Turkish, hoping to broaden the empire's intellectual horizons. He also welcomed scholars from Persia, the Arab world, and Europe, creating a diverse milieu that boosted the empire's prestige.

These cultural and religious policies aimed to integrate the varied populations of the expanding empire. Citizens of different faiths contributed to the empire's vitality, especially in trade, crafts, and scholarship. Tensions were inevitable, but Mehmed's approach generally avoided large-scale rebellions on religious grounds.

9. LATER YEARS AND FINAL CAMPAIGNS

Naval Ambitions

In his later reign, Mehmed II showed a growing interest in naval power. He recognized that controlling the seas was vital for projecting Ottoman influence in the Mediterranean. Though the empire had a fleet, it struggled to match the maritime republics of Venice or Genoa in naval expertise. Mehmed sought to modernize shipbuilding facilities, focusing on the **Golden Horn** docks in Istanbul. While progress was made, full naval dominance remained a work in progress.

Invasion of Italy?

One of Mehmed's most audacious dreams was to extend Ottoman rule into Italy, the seat of the Papacy and a symbolic center of Christian Europe. In 1480, Ottoman forces captured the Italian port of **Otranto**, raising alarm across the peninsula. However, Mehmed's death in 1481 and logistical challenges halted the campaign. Though the Ottomans withdrew, this episode demonstrated the sultan's far-reaching ambition.

10. DEATH OF MEHMED II AND HIS IMMEDIATE LEGACY

Passing of "The Conqueror"

Mehmed II died unexpectedly in 1481, near Gebze, while apparently preparing another military expedition—some say it was again directed toward Italy or Rhodes. News of his death was concealed briefly by court officials to prevent unrest until his son Bayezid could be informed. Despite his relatively short life (he was in his late forties), Mehmed had left an indelible mark on the empire.

Foundations for a World Power

By the time of Mehmed's death, the Ottoman Empire had transformed dramatically:

1. **Capital**: Istanbul (formerly Constantinople) was a thriving seat of power, bridging Europe and Asia.
2. **Administration**: Centralized structures governed a vast territory, with the sultan's authority reinforced by the Janissaries and a professional bureaucracy.
3. **Cultural Flourishing**: Artists, scholars, and architects converged in the new capital, reflecting Mehmed's broad intellectual curiosity.
4. **Continued Expansion**: Conquests spanned the Balkans, Anatolia, the Black Sea region, and outposts in the Aegean, setting the stage for future

Ottoman growth under sultans like Bayezid II, Selim I, and Suleiman the Magnificent.

11. CONCLUSION OF CHAPTER 8

Mehmed II's reign after 1453 was characterized by grand ambitions, strategic state-building, and a determination to elevate the Ottomans into a preeminent world power. The reforms he enacted—the promotion of centralized governance, legal codification, and cultural patronage—fundamentally reshaped the empire. His conquests expanded its borders significantly, and his transformation of Constantinople into Istanbul provided a vibrant core from which future sultans would rule.

In the chapters to come, we will examine how Mehmed's successors navigated the challenges and opportunities left behind. **Bayezid II**, Mehmed's son, would inherit a powerful realm but also face new tests at home and abroad. The foundational structures put in place by Mehmed II, however, would endure, ensuring that the Ottomans remained a dominant force in the Mediterranean and beyond for centuries.

CHAPTER 9

THE REIGN OF BAYEZID II AND SHIFTS IN POWER

When **Mehmed II ("the Conqueror")** died in 1481, the Ottoman Empire he left behind was powerful, centralized, and poised for further expansion. Yet transitions of power within the Ottoman dynasty were rarely smooth. **Bayezid II**, Mehmed's eldest surviving son, had to assert his claim against his brother Cem (pronounced "Jem") in a tense succession dispute. Once on the throne, Bayezid faced challenges both internal and external, ranging from the complexities of governing a diverse empire to dealing with Europe's rising naval powers. This chapter delves into Bayezid II's consolidation of authority, his policy directions, and how the empire adapted—or in some cases hesitated—to confront a changing political and economic landscape.

1. THE SUCCESSION STRUGGLE: BAYEZID II VS. PRINCE CEM

Mehmed II's Unexpected Death

Mehmed II's demise in 1481 came somewhat suddenly, leaving limited time to arrange a clear line of succession. Although the sultan had multiple sons, the principal rivals were Bayezid (governing Amasya) and Cem (governing Konya).

Upon receiving news of Mehmed's death, each prince raced to secure support among the military and the bureaucratic elites in Istanbul (Constantinople).

Cem's Bid for Power

Younger and more ambitious, Cem initially gained favor among some factions in Anatolia. However, the Janissaries and key viziers in the capital tended to support Bayezid, who they perceived as more stable and aligned with the empire's mainstream direction. After a series of skirmishes in Anatolia, Cem was forced to flee, eventually seeking refuge with the Knights of Rhodes and later at the courts of various European rulers, including the Papacy and the King of France.

Cem's exile became a diplomatic bargaining chip: European powers saw an opportunity to pressure Bayezid by threatening to unleash Cem as a rival claimant. Bayezid navigated this delicate situation by paying subsidies to keep Cem effectively under "house arrest" in Europe, thus preventing him from rallying Ottoman dissidents at home. Cem's eventual death (1495) ended the threat, though the financial and diplomatic toll of the episode lingered.

Bayezid's Consolidation

Victorious in the succession crisis, Bayezid II ascended the throne formally in 1481. One of his earliest tasks was to reward the Janissaries who had backed him. He issued generous bonuses—conforming to the established tradition that a new sultan grants a donative to secure military loyalty. Over time, Bayezid would come to rely heavily on the Janissaries, though this reliance was a double-edged sword: it strengthened the central army but made the sultan beholden to an increasingly powerful military corps.

2. BAYEZID'S PERSONALITY AND GOVERNING STYLE

A More Cautious Ruler

Where Mehmed II was driven, expansionist, and willing to take bold risks, Bayezid II is often depicted as more pious, reflective, and measured. He had a strong interest in theology, Sufism, and the arts. Although not opposed to military campaigns, he generally sought stability over conquest. This shift in temperament influenced the direction of Ottoman policies during his reign.

Balancing Internal and External Pressures

Bayezid inherited an empire that was culturally diverse and geographically vast. The central challenge was maintaining cohesion: local elites, religious minorities, and frontier lords all required careful governance. Meanwhile, the empire's frontiers touched competing powers—Venice in the Mediterranean, Hungary in the Balkans, the Mamluks in Syria and Egypt, and the growing Safavid influence in Persia.

In many respects, Bayezid's approach emphasized diplomacy, trade, and cautious military engagements. He did not neglect expansion entirely—he fought Venice, for instance—but he also avoided the large-scale conquests that had characterized Mehmed II's era. Some historians argue that Bayezid's more conservative stance gave the empire time to consolidate its recent gains, while others see it as a missed opportunity to push further into Europe or the Middle East.

3. INTERNAL REFORMS AND ADMINISTRATION

Financial Stability

With the empire's treasury strained by Mehmed II's ambitious projects and the prolonged handling of Prince Cem's situation, Bayezid focused on financial prudence. He introduced more systematic tax collection methods and undertook comprehensive surveys of timar holdings. Under his instructions, the Ottoman bureaucracy updated land registers (defter), ensuring accurate records of revenue streams. These measures helped replenish the treasury over time, supporting the standing army and public works without excessive new taxation.

Religious Patronage and Endowments

Bayezid is remembered for his strong religiosity. He funded mosque construction, schools (madrasas), and charitable foundations (waqfs) throughout the empire. Istanbul, Bursa, and Edirne saw the development of new religious complexes. These architectural endeavors served both devotional and political purposes: they legitimized Bayezid's rule, showcased Ottoman piety, and integrated newly conquered areas into the empire's cultural fabric.

The Role of the Ulema

During Bayezid's reign, the ulema (religious scholars) gained increased influence. Their backing was essential for maintaining public support, especially given Bayezid's own pious reputation. He appointed well-respected scholars as judges and muftis, integrating religious law (Sharia) more deeply into administrative affairs. This policy reduced friction between the state and conservative elements but also limited some of the secularizing impulses that had emerged under Mehmed II's Kanun-based reforms.

4. DIPLOMACY AND MILITARY ACTIONS IN THE BALKANS

Relations with Hungary

The Danube frontier remained a key zone of tension. Hungary, weakened by internal struggles, was not as formidable as it had been under Matthias Corvinus, but it still posed a potential threat. Bayezid occasionally launched raids or short campaigns to keep Hungarian forces on the defensive. However, no major offensive comparable to the siege of Belgrade (under Mehmed II) took place.

Instead, Bayezid preferred negotiating truces or alliances with smaller Balkan states, using vassalage or tributary arrangements. Serbia, Wallachia, and Bosnia all navigated these relationships. While not entirely stable, this approach minimized the risk of a broad anti-Ottoman coalition forming in the Balkans, allowing Bayezid to redirect resources as needed elsewhere.

The Venetian Rivalry

Venice remained a chief maritime rival. Commercial competition in the eastern Mediterranean was fierce, and territorial disputes flared over ports and islands. **The Ottoman-Venetian War (1499–1503)** was one of the more significant conflicts under Bayezid's rule. Ottoman forces, led by experienced admirals, targeted Venetian strongholds in the Ionian Sea.

Key victories, such as the Battle of Zonchio (1499), showcased the growing Ottoman naval prowess. Over time, Venice was forced to cede important territories, including ports along the Adriatic and Aegean seas. Though Venice remained a wealthy and formidable republic, it was compelled to adapt its strategies, recognizing the Ottomans as a dominant naval power in the region.

5. TENSIONS WITH THE MAMLUKS

Ottoman-Mamluk Rivalries

To the south, the **Mamluk Sultanate** controlled Syria, Egypt, and the Hejaz (including the Muslim holy cities of Mecca and Medina). Under Mehmed II, relations had been relatively peaceful, but competition over trade routes and influence in the Middle East simmered beneath the surface.

During Bayezid's reign, sporadic border clashes erupted in Cilicia (southern Anatolia) and near the Euphrates. Both sides courted local tribal leaders as proxies, hoping to destabilize the other's hold on frontier regions. However, a full-scale war did not break out until later. The delicate balance between the Ottomans and the Mamluks would eventually shift dramatically under Bayezid's successors, but in his time, the two powers mostly maintained a wary stalemate.

The Hajj Route and Pilgrim Caravans

One point of contention was the safety and control of pilgrimage routes to Mecca. The Mamluks, as guardians of the Hejaz, often claimed moral authority over the region's Muslims. Bayezid, seeking to bolster his Islamic credentials, sponsored caravan routes from Anatolia to Mecca, ensuring that pilgrims traveled under Ottoman protection. While this did not cause open conflict with the Mamluks, it foreshadowed a later struggle over who would claim leadership of the Islamic world.

6. THE RISE OF THE SAFAVIDS AND EASTERN PRESSURES

Emergence of Safavid Power

Perhaps the most transformative development during Bayezid II's reign was the rapid rise of the **Safavid dynasty** in Persia. Led by Shah Ismail, the Safavids championed Twelver Shi'a Islam, in contrast to the Ottoman Sunni orthodoxy. As the Safavids expanded from their base in Ardabil to conquer vast stretches of

Persia, their influence began to reach eastern Anatolia, where some local tribes and groups were receptive to Shi'a doctrines.

Kızılbaş Movements

Shah Ismail's followers, known as **Kızılbaş** ("Red Heads" due to their distinctive red headgear), spread propaganda and recruited supporters within Ottoman borders. This alarmed Bayezid, who feared the infiltration of a rival religious-political ideology. Tensions flared in Anatolian regions with large Turkmen populations, leading to sporadic rebellions.

Bayezid took measures to quell pro-Safavid sentiment, including exiling or executing suspected agitators. Still, these events foreshadowed a major Ottoman-Safavid confrontation under Bayezid's son, Selim I. The ideological divide between Sunni Ottomans and Shi'a Safavids would shape centuries of rivalry in the Middle East.

7. NAVAL EXPANSION AND EUROPEAN THREATS

The Ottoman Fleet's Growth

Mehmed II had initiated a push toward naval development, but it was under Bayezid II that the Ottoman fleet began to mature. The wars with Venice provided both the impetus and the practical experience needed. Bayezid's admirals introduced new ship designs, improved dockyards (especially in Galata and along the Aegean coast), and recruited skilled sailors.

This investment bore fruit not just in the Aegean but also in the Black Sea. Control over the Straits was critical for trade and military movement, and Bayezid ensured that Ottoman naval power could deter or respond to outside incursions. However, the empire was still learning to compete with seasoned maritime republics. Full mastery of the Mediterranean would only emerge in the following century under figures like Hayreddin Barbarossa during the reign of Suleiman the Magnificent.

Portuguese Expeditions

While the Ottomans focused on the eastern Mediterranean and Red Sea regions, European maritime powers—especially Portugal—were exploring new sea routes around Africa to reach India and beyond. Bayezid was well aware that these developments could diminish Ottoman control over lucrative spice and silk routes, which traditionally passed through the Middle East. Though not an immediate threat during his reign, these voyages hinted at a shifting global trade dynamic that would challenge Ottoman economic interests in the longer run.

8. NOTABLE INTERNAL INCIDENTS AND REVOLTS

The Shahkulu Rebellion

One significant revolt near the end of Bayezid II's rule was the **Shahkulu Rebellion (1511)** in southwestern Anatolia. Led by a charismatic dervish named Shahkulu, this uprising had religious and social dimensions. Many rebel followers were drawn from rural populations dissatisfied with heavy taxation and attracted by the Safavid message. Although the rebellion was eventually crushed, it underscored the growing tension between Ottoman Sunni orthodoxy and heterodox Shi'a movements.

Janissary Involvement in Palace Politics

As Bayezid aged, factionalism within the palace grew. The Janissaries, increasingly aware of their power, meddled in court affairs. They sometimes demanded higher pay or influenced the selection of high-level officials. This growing Janissary assertiveness would become a recurrent theme in later centuries, leading to periodic revolts that shaped Ottoman succession and governance.

9. PERSONAL LEGACY AND CHARACTER OF BAYEZID II

Patron of Learning and Arts

Even more than Mehmed II, Bayezid earned renown as a patron of scholars, poets, and artists. He commissioned major building projects in Istanbul and other cities, including mosques, libraries, and hospitals. Poets dedicated verses to him, praising his piety and generosity. Some historical accounts describe him as somewhat contemplative and cautious in worldly matters, while actively supporting mystics and Sufi orders.

The Humanitarian Gesture Toward Sephardic Jews

One of the most notable examples of Bayezid's tolerance and statesmanship was his welcoming of **Sephardic Jews** expelled from Spain in 1492 by the Catholic Monarchs, Ferdinand and Isabella. Bayezid is said to have remarked how unwise it was for the Spanish crown to drive out such productive citizens, and he invited them to settle in Ottoman lands. These Jewish refugees revitalized local economies, particularly in Salonica (Thessaloniki), Istanbul, and other urban centers, contributing to a cultural and economic renaissance.

The Aging Sultan

As Bayezid grew older, he relied more on his grand viziers and top military commanders. He showed little inclination to undertake major new conquests, focusing instead on domestic stability and religious patronage. This stance, while preserving peace in some regions, disappointed some who remembered Mehmed II's dynamic expansions. It also emboldened factions, particularly among the military, who sought a more aggressive foreign policy or who had personal ambitions tied to future leadership.

10. END OF BAYEZID II'S REIGN AND TRANSITION TO SELIM I

Succession Anxiety

Late in his reign, Bayezid II faced pressure from his sons, especially **Prince Selim** and **Prince Ahmed**, each vying to be recognized as the heir. Selim, ruling in Trebizond and later in the Kefe region (Crimea), was known for his martial vigor and suspicion of perceived threats like the Safavids. Ahmed, on the other hand, seemed more in line with Bayezid's moderate approach. The rivalry between these princes grew intense, with each courting the support of influential court factions and the Janissaries.

Janissary Support for Selim

Sensing Bayezid's weakening hold on the throne, the Janissaries increasingly backed Prince Selim, who promised higher pay and an aggressive campaign against the Safavids. In 1512, under pressure from Janissaries and facing Selim's open challenge, Bayezid reluctantly abdicated. He left Istanbul for retirement in Dimetoka but died shortly after, prompting rumors that he had been poisoned or died from the strain of political intrigues.

Assessment of Bayezid's Reign

Bayezid II governed during a period of relative peace and consolidation, a contrast to his father's aggressive expansion. He reinforced the empire's institutions, championed Islamic piety, and pursued alliances and diplomacy over warfare in many instances. Critics argue he missed opportunities for further conquest in Europe, while supporters highlight the empire's economic and cultural flourishing under his rule. Regardless, his abdication marked the end of an era of cautious stability, ushering in the rise of **Selim I**, whose reign would be defined by dramatic military campaigns and significant territorial acquisitions.

11. CONCLUSION OF CHAPTER 9

Bayezid II's reign stands as a vital bridge between Mehmed the Conqueror's sweeping transformations and the militant expansions of Selim I and Suleiman the Magnificent. In focusing on stability, cultural patronage, and diplomatic engagement, Bayezid allowed the empire to consolidate its earlier gains and strengthen its administrative frameworks. He supported religious scholarship and welcomed diverse communities, leaving a legacy of tolerance and growth in important urban centers.

Yet, the seeds of future strife were sown in the final years of his rule. The Janissaries grew bolder, the Safavid threat to the east loomed large, and discontent simmered among those who yearned for a more dynamic expansionist policy. As we move to the next chapter, we will see how **Selim I** decisively took the reins of power, embarking on campaigns that would reshape the empire's geography and set the stage for the unprecedented achievements of the 16th century.

CHAPTER 10

SELIM I (SELIM THE GRIM) AND EASTERN EXPANSION

When **Selim I** forced his father, Bayezid II, to abdicate in 1512, few anticipated the sweeping changes he would bring about in less than a decade. Nicknamed **"Yavuz"** (often translated as "the Grim" or "the Stern"), Selim reoriented the Ottoman Empire's strategic focus from the Balkans and the Aegean to the Middle East. His decisive victories over the Safavids in Persia and the Mamluks in Syria and Egypt drastically expanded Ottoman domains and altered the empire's religious and geopolitical identity. This chapter examines Selim's accession, the motivations behind his eastern campaigns, and the profound consequences of these conquests for the Ottoman state.

1. SELIM'S STRUGGLE FOR THE THRONE

Confrontation with Prince Ahmed

Selim's path to the throne was fraught with conflict. Bayezid II had shown favor to another son, **Prince Ahmed**, who governed parts of Anatolia with a moderate stance similar to Bayezid's. Selim, ruling from the Black Sea region, positioned himself as a champion of the empire's military interests and a bulwark against the growing Safavid threat.

The Janissaries, discontent with Bayezid's cautious policies, rallied to Selim, eager for renewed military action and the promises of booty and higher pay. When open clashes erupted between Selim and Ahmed's forces, Selim emerged victorious, capitalizing on his strong rapport with the standing army. He compelled Bayezid to abdicate and soon eliminated his brother's remaining power base. By 1513, Selim had consolidated control, ruthlessly dealing with any rivals within the family.

Early Moves to Secure Power

Selim quickly purged high-level officials suspected of loyalty to his father or Prince Ahmed. This created a climate of fear within the palace, but it also ensured a cohesive core of advisors loyal to the new sultan. He increased Janissary pay, reinforcing their bond and securing their crucial support for upcoming campaigns. The next step was a bold decision: to shift the empire's expansionist energies away from Europe and toward the East.

2. THE SAFAVID THREAT AND THE BATTLE OF CHALDIRAN

Ideological and Political Rivalry

The **Safavid Empire**, under Shah Ismail, posed more than just a territorial challenge. They championed Twelver Shi'ism, a branch of Islam fundamentally at odds with the Ottoman Sunni mainstream. Safavid agents (Kızılbaş) had stirred unrest in eastern Anatolia, challenging Ottoman authority. For Selim, the Safavids represented a heretical movement that threatened the religious unity and political stability of his empire.

Preparations for War

Determined to crush Shah Ismail, Selim spent months amassing a formidable army. He introduced further reforms to the Ottoman artillery and ensured his troops were well supplied. Selim famously sent letters to Ismail, demanding the Safavids cease their subversive activities and recognize Ottoman authority over border regions. Ismail, a charismatic leader celebrated as both a warrior and a mystic poet, dismissed Selim's threats with defiance.

The Battle of Chaldiran (1514)

The confrontation came to a head at **Chaldiran** (in modern-day Iran) on August 23, 1514. Selim's forces, estimated at around 100,000 strong, included highly disciplined Janissaries and advanced artillery. The Safavid cavalry, though brave and skilled at close combat, lacked heavy artillery. The Ottomans' superior firepower devastated the Safavid ranks, and Shah Ismail was forced to retreat.

The Ottoman victory at Chaldiran was decisive:

1. **Territorial Gains**: Selim annexed large parts of eastern Anatolia and northern Mesopotamia.
2. **Psychological Blow**: Shah Ismail's aura of invincibility was shattered, undermining Safavid prestige among their followers.
3. **Ottoman-Safavid Rivalry**: A new fault line emerged in the Islamic world—Sunni Ottomans vs. Shi'a Safavids—a rivalry that would last centuries.

3. AFTERMATH OF CHALDIRAN AND EASTERN REORGANIZATION

Occupation and Administration

Following Chaldiran, Selim's forces advanced on Tabriz, the Safavid capital. Although he did not hold the city for long, Selim's army looted its vast treasures, including manuscripts, artisans, and skilled workers. Some of these craftsmen were taken back to Istanbul, fueling an artistic and architectural bloom. Selim, however, deemed it too dangerous to push deeper into Persia with winter approaching and Safavid forces regrouping.

In the newly conquered provinces, the Ottoman administration set up local governors (beys and sancakbeys) loyal to Selim. Sunni Islam was promoted, though most local populations were given leeway as long as they did not openly support the Safavids. The frontier with Safavid Persia remained fluid, and skirmishes continued periodically, but Selim had effectively broken the Safavids' advance into Anatolia.

Dealing with Kızılbaş Influence

Inside Ottoman territory, Selim harshly repressed Kızılbaş sympathizers. He saw them as a fifth column for Safavid influence. Thousands were executed or exiled in the aftermath of Chaldiran, an event that remains controversial. The brutality underscored Selim's determination to maintain strict religious and political control. This period set a tone of deep-rooted hostility between the Ottoman state and certain heterodox communities in eastern Anatolia.

4. SHIFTING FOCUS TO THE MAMLUK SULTANATE

Reasons for Confrontation

Even before ascending the throne, Selim had recognized that the Mamluk Sultanate in Egypt and Syria was a key obstacle to Ottoman dominance in the Muslim world. The Mamluks controlled the holy cities of Mecca and Medina, as well as the lucrative trade routes from the Indian Ocean. They also maintained alliances with various Bedouin tribes in Arabia. By defeating the Mamluks, Selim could achieve multiple goals:

1. **Religious Prestige**: Controlling Mecca and Medina would elevate the Ottoman sultan's status as the protector of Islam's holiest sites.
2. **Trade Monopoly**: Direct control over Levantine ports and routes would strengthen Ottoman economic power.
3. **Elimination of a Rivalling Islamic Power**: The Mamluks, like the Safavids, could no longer undermine Ottoman authority if they were subjugated.

Diplomatic Breakdown

Initially, Selim tested the possibility of alliances or non-aggression pacts. However, Mamluk support for certain rebellious tribes, combined with lingering commercial disputes, made a settlement unlikely. By 1516, tensions reached a breaking point, and Selim prepared for a massive campaign southward, assembling artillery, cavalry, and thousands of Janissaries.

5. THE OTTOMAN–MAMLUK WARS (1516–1517)

Battle of Marj Dabiq (1516)

Selim's first major confrontation with the Mamluks took place at **Marj Dabiq**, near Aleppo in northern Syria, on August 24, 1516. The Mamluk army, noted for its elite cavalry, was formidable but outmatched by Ottoman gunpowder technology. Ottoman artillery pounded Mamluk lines, while disciplined Janissaries repelled cavalry charges. A key turning point was the death of the Mamluk sultan, Qansuh al-Ghuri, during the battle, plunging the Mamluk ranks into confusion.

The Ottomans emerged victorious, opening the path to Aleppo, Damascus, and eventually all of Syria. Local Syrian notables, faced with the unstoppable Ottoman advance, pledged loyalty to Selim. The sultan took care to present himself as a liberator rather than a conqueror, promising fair governance and protection of Islamic institutions.

Conquest of Cairo (1517)

After securing Syria, Selim advanced into Palestine and Egypt. The decisive clash came at **Ridaniya**, near Cairo, in January 1517. Though the Mamluks attempted to fortify defenses, they again failed to withstand Ottoman artillery and tactics. The new Mamluk sultan, Tuman Bay II, put up a brave fight but was eventually captured and executed. Cairo fell to the Ottomans, ending centuries of Mamluk rule.

With Egypt secured, Selim gained control over the Red Sea ports, the spice trade routes, and, crucially, the Hijaz. The Sharif of Mecca recognized Ottoman suzerainty, effectively granting Selim custodianship over Islam's holiest sites. This cemented the empire's religious legitimacy, a position that would profoundly influence Ottoman politics and identity for generations.

6. IMPACT ON THE ISLAMIC WORLD

Custodians of the Holy Cities

By taking control of Mecca and Medina, Selim I assumed the title of **"Servant of the Two Holy Sanctuaries"** (Hadimü'l-Haremeyn), reinforcing the Ottoman claim to be the leading Sunni Islamic power. The empire now safeguarded the pilgrimage routes, collected the surre (imperial endowments for the holy cities), and gained significant spiritual prestige.

The Caliphate and Symbolic Authority

A longstanding historical debate revolves around whether Selim officially assumed the title of **Caliph** after subjugating the Mamluks (who claimed a titular connection to the Abbasid caliphate in Cairo). While the precise details remain murky, over time the Ottomans increasingly presented themselves as inheritors of the caliphal mantle. This added a new dimension to their rule, blending Turkish sultanic authority with a universal Islamic leadership role.

7. ADMINISTERING NEW DOMAINS

Integrating Syria and Egypt

The newly conquered regions required swift administrative organization. Selim retained many local elites and bureaucrats in Syria and Egypt, ensuring continuity and reducing the risk of revolts. The Ottoman timar system was introduced selectively, but the complex landholding patterns in Egypt made direct transplantation difficult. Instead, a hybrid system emerged, combining local practices with Ottoman oversight.

Selim also stationed garrisons in major cities like Cairo and Damascus. Over time, these garrisons would integrate with local communities, though tensions occasionally flared between Ottoman soldiers and native populations. Nevertheless, the influx of Ottoman officials, merchants, and scholars brought new cultural and intellectual ties to these regions.

Safeguarding Maritime Routes

Control of the eastern Mediterranean and Red Sea became a priority. Selim's subjugation of the Mamluks allowed the Ottomans to fortify ports such as Alexandria and Suez, bolstering naval capabilities against any Portuguese encroachments in the Red Sea. Though full maritime dominance would require further expansions under later sultans, Selim's conquests laid the groundwork for an empire that extended its influence into the Indian Ocean trade networks.

8. INTERNAL CONSOLIDATION AND USE OF FORCE

Fear and Respect

Selim's rule was marked by an undercurrent of fear among the Ottoman elite. He relied on harsh measures to eliminate opposition. High-ranking officials who questioned his decisions or who were suspected of disloyalty often faced execution. While this policy consolidated his authority and removed threats, it also generated an atmosphere of suspicion at the Ottoman court.

Yet, Selim commanded immense respect from the military. His successes at Chaldiran, Marj Dabiq, and Ridaniya proved his strategic brilliance. Janissaries admired him for his decisive leadership, ensuring their loyalty. The sultan's willingness to share the spoils of war further cemented his bond with the army.

Ongoing Conflict with Kızılbaş

Despite the victory over the Safavids at Chaldiran, pro-Safavid sentiment lingered in eastern Anatolia. Selim continued his father's policy of suppressing heterodox sects. Thousands more were exiled, imprisoned, or executed. These actions reduced immediate revolts but sowed seeds of resentment that would manifest in later centuries as periodic uprisings.

9. FOREIGN RELATIONS AND LEGACY ABROAD

Relations with European Powers

Selim's campaigns were mostly oriented eastward, so he had limited direct confrontations with major European states. Nevertheless, news of his rapid conquests alarmed powers like Venice, Hungary, and the Papal States. They feared a renewed Ottoman thrust into Europe would follow. However, Selim died before turning his attention westward, leaving those future campaigns to his successor.

Still, the shift of Ottoman focus to the Middle East had repercussions in Europe. It gave frontier states along the Danube a temporary reprieve, though the threat of Ottoman expansion remained. Diplomatically, some European merchants sought concessions in newly conquered regions, recognizing that the spice trade routes now lay firmly in Ottoman hands.

Influence in the Muslim World

The downfall of the Mamluks and the checks placed on Safavid expansion elevated the Ottomans to an unrivaled position in the Islamic world. Cities like Cairo, once the center of Islamic scholarship under the Mamluks, adapted to Ottoman rule, fostering a blend of cultural influences. Scholars from across the Muslim world now sought patronage in Istanbul, aware that Selim's empire held the keys to the holy cities and the largest contiguous Muslim realm.

10. SELIM'S DEATH AND THE ASCENSION OF SULEIMAN

Final Campaigns and Sudden End

Selim's conquests had transformed the Ottoman world in just eight years (1512–1520). He planned further expansions, possibly aiming to consolidate control along the North African coast or even press deeper into Persia. However, in 1520, Selim died—some accounts suggest from illness such as cancer or a possibly lethal infection—while returning from a campaign in eastern Anatolia.

His death was sudden, and he left behind no prolonged succession crisis. His son, **Suleiman**, smoothly ascended the throne. Nicknamed "the Lawgiver" (Kanuni) by his subjects and "the Magnificent" by Europeans, Suleiman would inherit a vastly expanded empire, unprecedented in scope. Much of his future success built directly on the territorial and institutional groundwork laid by Selim.

Summary of Selim I's Achievements

Selim I's reign was short but transformative:

1. **Territorial Expansion**: He nearly doubled the empire's size by annexing Syria, Egypt, and the Arabian Peninsula's key territories.
2. **Religious Authority**: Possession of Mecca and Medina gave the Ottoman sultan unparalleled prestige in the Sunni Muslim world.
3. **Check on the Safavids**: By defeating Shah Ismail at Chaldiran, Selim contained Safavid influence and secured eastern Anatolia.

4. **Centralized Power**: Through ruthless purges and unwavering military backing, Selim reinforced the sultan's authority over provincial elites and the Janissaries.

11. CONCLUSION OF CHAPTER 10

Selim I is often remembered as the sultan who decisively shifted the Ottoman Empire's center of gravity to the Middle East. His triumphs over the Safavids and Mamluks were momentous, bringing sacred cities and critical trade routes under Ottoman sway. In less than a decade, he refashioned the empire into a major Sunni Islamic power with a vast expanse from the Danube to the Red Sea. Yet his methods—marked by severity and the suppression of dissent—earned him the epithet "the Grim."

In the next chapter, we will explore **the Golden Age under Suleiman the Magnificent**, where the empire reached new heights of territorial reach, cultural achievements, and administrative refinement. Selim's expansions set the stage, but it would be Suleiman who fully realized the Ottoman dream of a unified and influential Islamic superpower spanning three continents.

CHAPTER 11

THE GOLDEN AGE UNDER SULEIMAN THE MAGNIFICENT

When **Sultan Selim I** died in 1520, he left behind a massively expanded Ottoman Empire stretching from the Balkans deep into the Middle East and North Africa. His conquests had transformed the Ottomans into the leading power of the Muslim world. **Suleiman**, Selim's only surviving son, inherited this vast realm. Over the course of a long reign (1520–1566), Suleiman earned the moniker **"the Magnificent"** in Europe and **"Kanuni"** (the Lawgiver) among his subjects. This era is commonly referred to as the **Golden Age** of the Ottoman Empire due to its extensive territorial expansion, cultural achievements, and far-reaching legal and administrative reforms. In this chapter, we will explore Suleiman's ascent to power, his major military campaigns, the internal policies that defined his reign, and the cultural florescence that made the Ottoman Empire a leading center of art, architecture, and scholarship.

1. ACCESSION TO THE THRONE

Suleiman's Early Life

Born in 1494 (or 1495) in Trabzon, a city on the Black Sea coast, Suleiman spent much of his youth in provincial governorships—common practice for Ottoman princes. These roles prepared him for governance and familiarized him with the empire's administrative challenges. When his father, Selim I, died unexpectedly on his return from a campaign in 1520, Suleiman ascended the throne without facing a significant succession struggle, as he was Selim's only surviving heir.

In contrast to his father's stern reputation, Suleiman was described by contemporaries as thoughtful, well-educated, and curious about the arts and sciences. He was influenced by prominent advisors and tutors, including some who introduced him to Persian literature, Islamic jurisprudence, and world geography. Upon becoming sultan at about 25 or 26 years old, he brought a fresh perspective to the empire's leadership.

Early Consolidation

One of Suleiman's first actions was to secure the loyalty of the Janissaries, following the Ottoman tradition of providing a donative (cash gift) to the elite corps. He also confirmed key administrative personnel in their positions to ensure continuity. Nonetheless, expectations ran high. The empire had grown enormously during Selim's short reign, and many wondered if Suleiman could live up to that legacy or whether he would adopt a different path.

2. EUROPEAN EXPANSION: BELGRADE AND HUNGARY

Renewed Focus on the Balkans

Selim I had mostly turned eastward, subduing the Safavids and Mamluks. Suleiman, by contrast, revived the push into Europe. He saw opportunities in the unstable Balkan states and the longstanding conflict with the Kingdom of Hungary. Moreover, controlling the Danube region was vital for safeguarding the empire's European flank and guaranteeing trade routes.

The Capture of Belgrade (1521)

The Ottoman conquest of Belgrade in 1521 was a pivotal achievement. Located at the confluence of the Danube and Sava Rivers, Belgrade was a strategic fortress that blocked Ottoman penetration into central Europe. Earlier sultans, including Mehmed II, had tried to capture it without success. Suleiman's siege combined heavy artillery bombardment with a well-coordinated land and river blockade. After weeks of resistance, Belgrade capitulated, opening a clear path into the Hungarian heartland. This victory signaled Suleiman's serious intent to expand European territories.

The Battle of Mohács (1526)

The next major milestone came in 1526 at the **Battle of Mohács**, fought against the forces of King Louis II of Hungary. Ottoman artillery and disciplined Janissaries overwhelmed the outnumbered Hungarian army on the plains of southern Hungary. In a chaotic retreat, King Louis II was killed, and Hungarian national defenses collapsed. Mohács is often cited as the death knell for medieval Hungary, leading to a power vacuum in the region.

In the aftermath, Suleiman occupied Buda (part of modern-day Budapest), dividing Hungarian factions into those who recognized Ottoman suzerainty and those who aligned with the Habsburgs in Austria. This set the stage for a protracted rivalry between the Ottomans and the Habsburg Monarchy over control of central Europe. Although Suleiman did not permanently annex all of Hungary at this time, the battle established the Ottomans as a dominant force in the region.

3. CLASH WITH THE HABSBURG MONARCHY

The Siege of Vienna (1529)

Bolstered by successes in Hungary, Suleiman led a campaign toward Vienna in 1529. The Habsburg capital presented a formidable challenge. The Ottomans reached the city later in the season than planned, and heavy rains and logistical issues weakened their siege efforts. Despite pounding Vienna's walls, the Ottomans could not breach the city before winter approached. Suleiman withdrew, marking the first failed Ottoman attempt to capture Vienna. While the campaign showcased the empire's reach, it also highlighted supply and weather constraints that would shape future military planning.

Continued Rivalry

Over the next decades, the Ottomans and the Habsburgs engaged in back-and-forth contests, especially in the divided territories of Hungary. Some sections recognized an Ottoman vassal king, while others allied with the Habsburgs. Although a definitive conquest of Austria eluded Suleiman, his repeated campaigns established a long frontier along the Danube and introduced a tense balance of power. Diplomatic negotiations interspersed with military clashes, foreshadowing centuries of Ottoman–Habsburg rivalry in southeastern Europe.

4. WARFARE IN THE EAST: SAFAVID PERSIA

Ongoing Sunni-Shi'a Conflict

Despite his focus on Europe, Suleiman did not neglect the eastern frontier. The Safavid Empire, ruled now by Shah Tahmasp (successor to Ismail), remained a rival in matters of territory and ideology. Safavid influence in eastern Anatolia and the Caucasus threatened Ottoman control over vital trade routes. Both empires competed for the allegiance of local tribes and sought to expand their sphere of influence at the other's expense.

Campaigns Under Suleiman

Suleiman launched multiple campaigns into Safavid territory:

1. **1533–1535 Campaign**: Led to the temporary capture of Tabriz and Baghdad, bringing important cultural and trade centers under Ottoman rule.
2. **1548–1549 and 1553–1555 Campaigns**: Resulted in seesaw battles for control of Azerbaijan and Iraq. Suleiman's forces gained Baghdad permanently and established a stronger Ottoman presence in Mesopotamia.

The Peace of Amasya (1555)

Eventually, both empires recognized the limits of their resources and signed the **Peace of Amasya** in 1555. This treaty defined borders: the Ottomans retained control of Baghdad, much of Mesopotamia, and parts of the Caucasus, while the Safavids held on to the core of Persia. Though not eliminating rivalry, the treaty introduced a period of relative calm. It also allowed Suleiman to direct more energy toward Europe and the Mediterranean maritime theatre.

5. NAVAL EXPANSION: THE MEDITERRANEAN AND BEYOND

The Rise of the Ottoman Navy

Under Suleiman, the Ottoman Empire became a key naval power. Building on reforms begun under Bayezid II, the fleet rapidly expanded. Skilled admirals such as **Hayreddin Barbarossa** (an Algerian privateer who entered Ottoman service) spearheaded maritime campaigns. Ottoman shipyards in Istanbul and Gallipoli launched modern galleys and other warships, competing with the naval arsenals of Venice and Genoa.

Key Victories

- **Conquest of Rhodes (1522)**: Secured the eastern Mediterranean by dislodging the Knights Hospitaller. Their well-fortified island had blocked Ottoman shipping routes to the Levant. Suleiman personally oversaw the siege, which ended in the Knights' departure for Malta.
- **Algerian and North African Expeditions**: Barbarossa's actions brought Algiers, Tunis, and other coastal territories under varying degrees of Ottoman sovereignty. This expansion gave the empire a foothold in the western Mediterranean.
- **Clashes with the Habsburgs in the Sea**: The Ottomans battled Spanish fleets in the western Mediterranean. Although neither side achieved outright dominance, Ottoman control of the central and eastern Mediterranean grew, bolstering trade and troop movements.

Indian Ocean Forays

Suleiman also sent naval expeditions into the Red Sea and Persian Gulf to challenge Portuguese encroachments. Though limited in scope compared to Mediterranean campaigns, these efforts protected Ottoman interests in Mecca and Medina and secured partial control over spice routes from the Indian Ocean to the Middle East.

6. DOMESTIC REFORMS: SULEIMAN THE LAWGIVER

Central Administration and the Kanun

Suleiman's epithet "Kanuni" (Lawgiver) arose from his comprehensive legal reforms. He promulgated **Kanun** (sultanic law) that supplemented Islamic Sharia in areas like taxation, land tenure, and criminal justice. These laws unified administrative practices across the empire's diverse provinces, reducing corruption and clarifying the rights and obligations of subjects. Suleiman's codification built on Mehmed II's earlier efforts but expanded them, ensuring more consistent governance from the Balkans to Egypt.

The Role of the Grand Vizier

Central to these reforms was an evolving bureaucracy led by the **Grand Vizier**. Suleiman appointed capable statesmen, most famously **Pargalı Ibrahim Pasha**, who served as Grand Vizier in the 1520s and 1530s. Ibrahim's reforms streamlined the tax system, enhanced the timar (land grant) arrangements, and restructured the judicial system. Although Ibrahim's downfall later in the reign demonstrated the perils of accumulating power too quickly, the administrative blueprint he helped create endured beyond his tenure.

The Millet System

While the millet system—where non-Muslim communities managed their own religious affairs under Ottoman oversight—had precedent, Suleiman refined it. Christian and Jewish communities maintained their patriarchs or chief rabbis, who acted as intermediaries with the state. This policy helped maintain stability in conquered territories by permitting cultural and religious autonomy, as long as taxes were paid and Ottoman authority was respected.

7. CULTURAL AND ARCHITECTURAL FLORESCENCE

Mimar Sinan and Imperial Architecture

The Suleiman era is famous for monumental architecture, much of it shaped by the legendary chief architect **Mimar Sinan**. A devşirme recruit of Greek or Armenian origin, Sinan served as an army engineer before leading imperial construction projects. His works included mosques, bridges, aqueducts, and other public structures that combined aesthetic grace with practical functionality.

- **Süleymaniye Mosque (1550–1557)**: Built on one of Istanbul's hills overlooking the Golden Horn, it became a symbol of imperial grandeur. Its large dome, balanced courtyard, and supporting complexes (madrasas, soup kitchens, and hospitals) exemplified Sinan's architectural genius.
- **Other Projects**: Sinan designed or improved major constructions across the empire, from Edirne to Damascus, ensuring Ottoman architectural patronage extended far and wide.

Arts, Literature, and Patronage

Suleiman himself was a poet, writing under the pen name **Muhibbi**. His court hosted scholars, calligraphers, painters, and musicians from various cultural backgrounds. The imperial treasury funded translations of classic texts, while workshops in Istanbul and other cities produced exquisite ceramics (Iznik ware), carpets, and metalwork. This cultural fusion merged Persian, Byzantine, Arab, and Turkish influences, giving Ottoman arts a distinctive flavor.

8. COURT LIFE AND SUCCESSION CONCERNS

The Influence of Hürrem Sultan (Roxelana)

A defining aspect of Suleiman's private life was his relationship with **Hürrem Sultan**, known in Europe as Roxelana. Originally a slave concubine from Eastern Europe, she rose to become Suleiman's legal wife—an unprecedented move in Ottoman tradition, which typically discouraged sultans from formal marriage. Hürrem became highly influential in court politics, founding charitable institutions and shaping diplomatic endeavors. Though admired by some, she was also viewed with suspicion, especially by those who resented her sway over the sultan.

Family Rivalries

Suleiman's reign was not free from internal intrigue. Ottoman succession customs allowed each prince to vie for the throne, often leading to lethal rivalries. The most tragic case involved **Prince Mustafa**, Suleiman's eldest and highly popular son, who was accused of plotting against his father. Influenced by palace advisors—and possibly by Hürrem's faction—Suleiman ordered Mustafa's execution in 1553, a decision that shocked the army and populace. This event underlined the darker side of the imperial household, where suspicion could override family bonds.

9. DIPLOMATIC RELATIONS AND THE "CAPITULATIONS"

Alliances and Envoys

During Suleiman's rule, the empire became deeply integrated into European power dynamics. Ambassadors from France, Venice, and other states frequented the Ottoman court, seeking trade privileges or military alliances. In a notable development, France secured **"capitulations"** (commercial and legal privileges) in Ottoman domains. These agreements exempted French merchants from some local taxes and legal constraints, fostering a lucrative trade network. Suleiman aimed to use such alliances to counterbalance Habsburg influence, effectively playing European powers against each other.

Exchange of Letters

Suleiman communicated with Western monarchs as an equal—or even as a superior figure. His correspondence with King Francis I of France showcased shifting alliances where both sides saw mutual benefits. Francis needed Ottoman pressure on the Habsburgs to safeguard French interests, while Suleiman welcomed a diplomatic hedge that further isolated Austria. Such exchanges highlight the global reach of the empire, which confidently negotiated with Christian Europe on its own terms.

10. THE FINAL YEARS OF SULEIMAN AND HIS LEGACY

Later Military Campaigns

In the closing decade of Suleiman's reign, he continued to command military campaigns despite advanced age and ill health. He captured strategic fortresses like Szigetvár in 1566, in a grueling siege. However, during this campaign, the sultan died in his military tent—his death was kept secret for a short time to prevent a collapse in morale.

The fate of Szigetvár, which the Ottomans finally took, mirrored the empire's unstoppable push, but the sultan's demise also symbolized the end of a monumental era. By the time news reached Istanbul, statesmen had already begun ensuring a smooth succession for **Selim II**, Suleiman's surviving son.

Assessment of the Golden Age

Under Suleiman, the empire reached its geographic zenith, spanning from Algeria's coast to the Persian Gulf, and from the southern edges of the Arabian

Peninsula to the gates of Vienna. The sultan's legal codifications strengthened internal unity, while his patronage of art and architecture left an indelible cultural legacy. This period stands out not only for military might but also for administrative sophistication and cultural blending, which would influence Ottoman society for generations.

Suleiman's reign did face challenges: fierce competition for power within the palace, the burden of near-constant warfare, and the seeds of future economic strains—like inflation from new world silver. Still, he is generally remembered as one of the empire's most successful and enlightened rulers, presiding over what many historians consider its true golden age.

11. CONCLUSION OF CHAPTER 11

Suleiman the Magnificent's era transformed the Ottoman Empire into a preeminent power, admired and feared across continents. His conquests in central Europe, the Middle East, and the Mediterranean secured unparalleled territorial gains. His legal and administrative reforms, coupled with extensive cultural patronage, earned him the dual legacy of a mighty conqueror and a thoughtful lawgiver.

In the next chapter, **Chapter 12: Later Reigns of the 16th Century and Internal Developments**, we will explore how the empire's leadership after Suleiman managed—or sometimes struggled—to sustain this golden legacy. As the century drew to a close, shifting global trade patterns, mounting military costs, and evolving political structures began to challenge the empire's stability, setting the stage for debates on "decline" and transformation that would surface in the following centuries.

CHAPTER 12

LATER REIGNS OF THE 16TH CENTURY AND INTERNAL DEVELOPMENTS

Following **Suleiman the Magnificent's** death in 1566, the Ottoman Empire retained much of its power and prestige, but the path ahead was increasingly uncertain. Shifts in warfare, global trade, and internal governance challenged the empire's status quo. This chapter examines the latter half of the 16th century, focusing on the reigns of **Selim II** (1566–1574), **Murad III** (1574–1595), and the early years of **Mehmed III** (1595–1603). It also investigates how the empire navigated changing economic pressures, evolving administrative practices, and external conflicts—particularly with European powers and the Safavid Persians. Although this period remains overshadowed by Suleiman's achievements, it laid crucial groundwork for the empire's transition into the 17th century.

1. SELIM II: A CHANGE IN STYLE

Accession of Selim II

When Suleiman died at the Siege of Szigetvár in 1566, his son **Selim II** ascended smoothly, partly because all rival princes had been eliminated. Nicknamed **"Selim the Sot"** by some European observers due to rumors of indulgence in wine, Selim II presented a notable contrast to his father. He was less personally involved in military campaigns and relied heavily on powerful advisors and the military bureaucracy.

Shift in Governance

Under Selim II, the role of the **Grand Vizier** and other high-ranking officials grew more prominent. Men like **Sokollu Mehmed Pasha** became pivotal in managing state affairs. Sokollu Mehmed was an experienced bureaucrat who aimed to continue Suleiman's policies, maintaining the empire's stability and controlling its far-flung territories. During this time, the sultan spent more of his reign in the capital, delegating day-to-day governance, a pattern that would gradually become more common among later sultans.

2. MILITARY CAMPAIGNS AND NAVAL ENCOUNTERS

Cyprus and the War with Venice

Selim II's most significant military venture was the **conquest of Cyprus** from Venice (1570–1571). Cyprus was a strategically located island in the eastern Mediterranean, vital for regional trade. The Ottomans quickly captured Nicosia, but Famagusta held out for almost a year. When it finally fell, the Venetians were forced to negotiate terms, ceding Cyprus to the Ottomans. However, the conflict drew in a Christian coalition that aimed to challenge Ottoman naval supremacy.

The Battle of Lepanto (1571)

In response to the Ottoman expansion in the Mediterranean, a Holy League—comprising Spain, Venice, the Papal States, and others—assembled a large fleet. This coalition decisively defeated the Ottoman navy in the **Battle of Lepanto** in October 1571, near western Greece. The encounter is renowned for being one of the largest naval battles of oared ships in history. Although the Ottomans quickly rebuilt their fleet, Lepanto shattered the myth of Ottoman naval invincibility. From this point forward, the empire had to share maritime power in the Mediterranean with European states.

Aftermath and Assessment

Despite the Lepanto defeat, the Ottomans retained Cyprus and regained enough naval strength to keep a major presence in the eastern Mediterranean. Yet the battle signaled a shift: European powers, particularly Spain, Venice, and later Portugal, were advancing in naval technology and exploration. The Ottomans still commanded respect, but they no longer appeared unstoppable at sea.

3. INTERNAL CHALLENGES AND SOCIOECONOMIC PRESSURES

Inflation and the Price Revolution

A significant global factor affecting the late 16th-century Ottoman economy was the **Price Revolution**—a term describing widespread inflation partly caused by the influx of silver from the Americas into Europe. As silver flooded European markets, it altered global prices, and the Ottoman Empire, integrated into European trade networks, felt the impact. The prices of essential goods soared, wages lagged, and the treasury had to manage currency devaluation. These changes placed pressure on the peasantry and the timar-holding sipahis, who found their incomes unable to keep pace with rising costs.

Corruption and Provincial Discontent

Some provincial governors and tax farmers exploited the situation, extracting higher taxes from peasants to offset their own losses from inflation. Reports of local rebellions or banditry (known as **"celali revolts"** in Anatolia) grew more frequent. Although these uprisings were sporadic, they hinted at a deeper structural problem: the empire's economic framework, designed for a less monetized age, struggled under mounting fiscal pressures.

4. MURAD III (1574–1595) AND CONTINUED STRAINS

A More Secluded Sultan

When **Selim II** died in 1574, **Murad III** took the throne. He inherited a system increasingly reliant on viziers and harem politics. Murad spent much of his reign within the Topkapı Palace walls, involving himself intermittently in state affairs. He was interested in arts and religious matters but left strategic decision-making largely to his grand viziers and influential court figures.

War with Safavids Resumes

Under Murad III, hostilities with the **Safavids** flared again. The Peace of Amasya (1555) had kept the eastern frontier relatively calm for two decades, but new disputes over control of the Caucasus and Baghdad rekindled conflict. While the Ottomans enjoyed some victories early on, the long and drawn-out campaigns in the 1580s and 1590s placed additional burdens on the treasury and the army. Maintaining supply lines and paying troops became more challenging as inflation gnawed at state resources.

The Long Turkish War in Europe

In tandem with eastern wars, tensions along the Habsburg frontier persisted. Known as the **Long Turkish War** (1593–1606), this protracted struggle between the Ottomans and the Habsburgs further drained Ottoman finances. Campaigns in Hungary and Croatia required large armies year after year, diminishing the sultan's ability to focus on internal governance or implement lasting reforms.

5. THE IMPACT OF COURT POLITICS AND THE HAREM

Growth of the Harem's Influence

During Murad III's reign, the imperial harem gained unprecedented political leverage. Royal consorts, princesses, and the sultan's mother (Valide Sultan) wielded power behind the scenes, engaging in patronage, charity, and at times, factional maneuvering. This phenomenon, sometimes labeled the **"Sultanate of Women"** by modern historians, reflected broader shifts: as sultans became more secluded, female members of the dynasty and high-ranking eunuchs filled advisory gaps.

Eunuchs and Palace Hierarchy

Eunuchs, especially the **Chief Black Eunuch**, managed daily operations within the harem and oversaw communication with the outside world. Their role grew in significance when the sultan was less active in governance. Some eunuchs formed alliances with powerful viziers, creating intricate palace power blocs that shaped appointments and resource distribution.

6. CONTINUITY IN ART AND CULTURE

Artistic Patronage Despite Turmoil

Even with economic and political strains, the late 16th century remained culturally vibrant. Sultans, viziers, and influential women commissioned mosques, schools, and public fountains. Miniature painting flourished, with court artists producing detailed manuscripts that depicted Ottoman victories, royal ceremonies, and everyday life.

Literary Trends

Poetry still held an esteemed place in elite culture. Writers composed verses in Ottoman Turkish, Persian, and Arabic, catering to diverse readerships. Historiography also advanced, as chroniclers documented the empire's wars, court intrigues, and social conditions. This period witnessed a blend of nostalgia for Suleiman's golden era and concern over present challenges, themes that threaded through many literary works.

7. ADMINISTRATIVE RESPONSES TO CRISIS

Attempts at Reform

Some grand viziers recognized the need to address rising corruption and fiscal shortfalls. They proposed reforms aimed at regulating tax farming, restoring the timar system's integrity, and controlling janissary expansion. However, implementing these policies proved difficult given entrenched interests. The Janissaries, for instance, resisted any changes that might reduce their stipends or privileges.

The Devşirme and Janissary Evolution

Although the **devşirme** system continued, the profile of Janissary recruits changed over time. More often, sons of existing Janissaries or urban families found ways into the elite corps, eroding the original concept of forcibly conscripting rural Christian youths. This shift reduced the sense of separation between the Janissaries and the broader population, complicating discipline and the corps' loyalty to the sultan alone.

8. MEHMED III (1595–1603) AND THE END OF THE CENTURY

Harsh Succession Practices

When Murad III died in 1595, his son **Mehmed III** ascended amid renewed security concerns. In line with Ottoman succession traditions that had grown more brutal, Mehmed III reportedly executed his younger brothers upon taking the throne to prevent any future rival claims. This action, while grim, demonstrated how the fear of dynastic disputes still dominated Ottoman political life.

Continued Military Engagement

Mehmed III immediately faced intense pressure in the **Long Turkish War** against the Habsburgs. While the Ottomans scored some victories—such as capturing Eger (Eğri) in 1596—conflicts dragged on, draining finances and manpower. Meanwhile, the Safavid front, though quieter, remained unsettled.

The Jelali Revolts

In Anatolia, tax burdens and mismanagement fueled larger-scale **Jelali rebellions**. Local chieftains and bandit leaders capitalized on peasant discontent, challenging provincial authorities. Although not unified under a single ideology, these uprisings reflected a broader sense of crisis. Mehmed III's government adopted harsh measures to quell the rebellions, but their recurrence hinted at deeper economic and social fractures.

9. EUROPEAN RELATIONS AND DIPLOMACY

Growing Presence of Other Powers

By the late 16th century, England and the Dutch Republic had begun to show interest in forging commercial relations with the Ottomans. Hoping to access Middle Eastern markets and bypass Spanish-dominated sea routes, these powers negotiated "capitulations," akin to the agreements France enjoyed. The empire cautiously welcomed these new partnerships, seeing them as a way to counter Habsburg and Venetian influence. However, the expanding web of European maritime trade also signaled a potential shift in global commercial routes that would challenge traditional Ottoman trade corridors.

Military Technology Gaps

While the Ottomans still fielded large, disciplined armies, European states were rapidly innovating in gun-making, fortifications, and naval engineering. Spanish and Italian fortification styles spread across Europe, introducing star forts and bastions that made sieges more difficult. The Ottomans tried to keep pace, but the empire's vast size sometimes hindered the quick adoption of the latest methods in all provinces. This gradual gap in military innovation would become more pronounced in the 17th century.

10. REFLECTIONS ON THE LATE 16TH CENTURY

Signs of Transformation

By 1600, the Ottoman Empire was still a dominant power, ruling diverse lands with a formidable army and navy. Yet cracks had begun to surface. Inflation, rebellious provinces, factionalism at court, and the challenge of maintaining two major frontiers (against the Habsburgs and the Safavids) weighed heavily on the state. The administrative and military framework designed during the empire's swift expansion now faced strains in a changing geopolitical environment.

The Concept of "Decline"

Later historians often labeled this period as the start of an Ottoman "decline." Modern scholarship, however, questions that blanket term. Instead, many scholars suggest the empire was **transforming**—shifting from a rapid-conquest machine to a more bureaucratic state that had to adapt to worldwide economic changes and evolving technologies. The empire's internal dynamics—like the rising power of the palace harem, the partial breakdown of the devşirme system, and the complexities of tax farming—indicate a move away from earlier models rather than a simple collapse of capabilities.

The Road Ahead

As the 17th century dawned, the Ottomans would face more profound challenges: drawn-out wars, fiscal crises, and a kaleidoscope of external pressures. Yet they also proved resilient, finding new ways to govern and harness resources. The innovations and crises of the late 16th century would shape that trajectory, setting the stage for further reforms under influential grand viziers and sultans who tried to revitalize the empire.

11. CONCLUSION OF CHAPTER 12

The later half of the 16th century saw the Ottoman Empire maintain its status as a major world power but also grapple with growing internal and external pressures. Selim II and Murad III governed through strong viziers and palace intermediaries, while Lepanto (1571) demonstrated that Ottoman naval supremacy could be challenged. Socioeconomic strains—most notably inflation and local uprisings—exposed structural flaws in the empire's traditional systems of taxation and military service. Yet, cultural patronage continued, and new commercial relationships with emerging European states hinted at fresh economic possibilities.

By the century's close, under Mehmed III, the empire was engaged in costly wars on multiple fronts, and the seeds of future unrest—like the Jelali revolts—were clearly visible. Nonetheless, the empire's robust institutions and proven adaptability gave it a measure of stability. In the chapters ahead, we will see how 17th-century rulers and grand viziers attempted to revitalize, reform, or at times merely survive within the evolving global and regional landscape.

CHAPTER 13

DECLINE? REASSESSING THE 17TH CENTURY

By the dawn of the 17th century, the Ottoman Empire was still a formidable power spanning three continents. Yet it was also evident that the empire faced new challenges and uncertainties. The term **"decline"** has often been used by historians to describe this era, implying that the empire's best days were behind it after the death of Süleyman the Magnificent. However, modern scholarship argues that this period is more complex than a simple downward trajectory. Multiple wars, internal power struggles, economic fluctuations, and changing administrative structures shaped the Ottoman experience during the 17th century. In this chapter, we will explore how the empire navigated its many pressures, how different sultans and grand viziers attempted to adapt, and why the notion of "decline" may not capture the entire reality of this transformative century.

1. DEFINING THE 17TH CENTURY CONTEXT

Transitional Era or Straight Decline?

The empire in the 1600s still commanded respect. Major cities like Istanbul, Cairo, and Aleppo thrived as trade and cultural centers. The military could still field large, well-organized armies, and the Ottoman navy maintained presence in the Mediterranean and Red Sea. However, several issues converged:

1. **Administrative Shifts**: Sultans becoming more secluded, palace factions gaining influence.
2. **Economic Challenges**: Inflation, mercantile competition from European sea powers, and disruptions to traditional land-based trade routes.
3. **Military Evolution**: Need for more modern tactics and technology, especially given rising European fortification and artillery developments.
4. **Provincial Unrest**: Recurring rebellions in Anatolia (the Jelali revolts), tensions in the Arab provinces, and difficulties managing distant territories in North Africa and the Balkans.

While some interpret these as signs of a general decline, others view them as natural transitions faced by a large empire adapting to global changes.

Succession of Sultans and Power Structures

The early 17th century saw rapid changes on the throne. Sultans like **Ahmed I** (1603–1617), **Mustafa I** (1617–1618, and again 1622–1623), **Osman II** (1618–1622), and **Murad IV** (1623–1640) each faced internal court intrigues and external threats. The frequent turnover sometimes destabilized governance. The imperial harem, especially the role of the sultan's mother (Valide Sultan) and the chief eunuchs, became increasingly pivotal in shaping policy and succession.

2. THE REIGNS OF EARLY 17TH-CENTURY SULTANS

Ahmed I (1603–1617) and the Blue Mosque

Ascending the throne at a young age, Ahmed I sought to restore prestige after a series of costly wars. Notable for commissioning the **Sultan Ahmed Mosque** (popularly known as the **Blue Mosque**) in Istanbul, he also attempted to rein in corruption. Ahmed abolished the practice of fratricide, replacing it with a system where princes were kept in a kind of guarded seclusion known as the **Kafes** (Cage). Though well-intentioned in preserving family members, this system produced future sultans with limited political experience.

Ahmed's era was not free of problems. The Celali revolts persisted in Anatolia, and the empire was engaged in conflicts with the Habsburgs and the Safavids. Nonetheless, Ahmed I left a cultural and architectural legacy that endures in modern Istanbul.

Osman II (1618–1622) and a Youthful Reformer

Osman II came to power as a teenager, displaying ambition to revitalize the military and administration. Concerned about the Janissaries' growing influence, he planned to create a new loyal army from Anatolia and beyond. Osman also attempted financial reforms to restore the treasury. However, his abrupt moves and perceived arrogance alienated key power blocs—most notably the Janissaries.

In 1622, the Janissaries revolted, deposed, and eventually executed Osman II. This shocking event underlined the Janissaries' capacity to dominate palace politics, punishing any sultan who threatened their privileges. It further reinforced the image of an empire plagued by internal strife, though many of these power struggles were typical of large states adjusting to new social and military realities.

Murad IV (1623–1640): A Harsh Restorer of Order

Following the crisis of Osman II's reign, Murad IV ascended as a child. Initially, the empire was effectively governed by factional interests and the regency of his relatives. By his late teens, Murad took control with an iron fist. He ruthlessly suppressed rebellions, executed corrupt officials, and curbed Janissary excesses. He famously banned tobacco, coffeehouses, and certain social gatherings he saw as breeding grounds for sedition.

Murad's successes included the reconquest of Baghdad from the Safavids in 1638, restoring Ottoman authority in parts of Mesopotamia. Although his methods were brutal—earning him a reputation similar to Selim I—Murad stabilized the empire's internal situation for a time. His untimely death in 1640 left a mixed legacy: an empire re-secured militarily but still vulnerable to future internal rifts.

3. WOMEN'S POWER AND THE "SULTANATE OF WOMEN"

Kösem Sultan and Valide Influence

During the early and mid-17th century, figures like **Kösem Sultan** (the mother of Murad IV and later of Ibrahim I) wielded significant power. Serving as Valide Sultan (Queen Mother), Kösem influenced appointments, brokered alliances among court factions, and even arranged marriages for princesses to key military or administrative leaders. This phenomenon, sometimes called the **Sultanate of Women**, reflected a shift in power dynamics as sultans were often minors or unprepared for direct rule.

Public Perception

Some contemporaries criticized the ascendancy of royal women, accusing them of furthering nepotism and corruption. Others acknowledged the Valide Sultan's role in stabilizing the throne during periods of chaos. These women also sponsored charitable works, including mosques, soup kitchens, and schools, tying their reputations to piety and public welfare. The interplay between harem politics and state governance remains one of the most debated aspects of 17th-century Ottoman life.

4. ECONOMIC AND SOCIAL DISRUPTIONS

Agriculture and Taxation

The empire's agrarian base faced repeated shocks. Ongoing wars devastated harvests and disrupted trade routes. Government attempts to raise extra revenue often resulted in over-taxation, pushing peasants to migrate or rebel. Some sought refuge in bandit groups or joined local warlords, exacerbating the Celali uprisings in Anatolia.

Meanwhile, the **timar** system, which traditionally provided cavalry with land grants in exchange for service, deteriorated. Fewer timar lands were available, and more positions were sold to tax farmers who squeezed peasants for maximum profit. This commercialization undermined the old military-land structure, sowing resentment and weakening the once-reliable provincial cavalry (sipahis).

Urban Growth and Guild Pressures

Major cities like Istanbul, Cairo, and Aleppo continued to expand, attracting migrants from rural areas seeking work or fleeing unrest. Urban guilds—representing bakers, butchers, textile workers, and others—negotiated with state officials over price controls and taxes. The state, aiming to ensure stable food supplies, imposed strict price regulations on staples like bread. At times, tensions flared between guilds and local governors over resources and competition from imported goods.

5. WARFARE AND DIPLOMACY

Continued Struggles with the Habsburgs

Though the Long Turkish War (1593–1606) ended in stalemate, skirmishes flared intermittently along the Danube frontier throughout the 17th century. Periodic peace treaties with the Habsburgs stabilized certain border regions but rarely lasted long. Both sides were under strain: the Ottomans grappled with internal revolts and administrative changes, while the Habsburgs faced religious conflicts and challenges within the Holy Roman Empire. This mutual exhaustion sometimes produced pragmatic truces rather than decisive conquests.

Rivalry with the Safavids

The Ottoman-Safavid rivalry continued through the century, revolving around control of Baghdad, the Caucasus, and eastern Anatolia. Although Murad IV's recapture of Baghdad in 1638 was a significant Ottoman victory, the region remained a flashpoint. Diplomatic efforts, including occasional marriages between noble families, sometimes calmed tensions, but fundamental sectarian and geopolitical differences lingered. The Treaty of Zuhab (1639) stabilized borders for a generation, but local conflicts and tribal allegiances often disrupted the nominal peace.

Naval Affairs: Mediterranean and Beyond

Ottoman naval presence in the Mediterranean faced challenges from growing European maritime powers. Spain, France, and later England and the Netherlands expanded their fleets. The Ottomans held strategic ports like Tunis, Algiers, and Tripoli through semi-autonomous regencies, relying on corsairs and local militias to maintain dominance. Conflicts with the Knights of Malta and repeated skirmishes near Crete and other islands showcased an ongoing competition for sea lanes.

In the Red Sea and the Indian Ocean, the Ottomans clashed with Portuguese forces over control of spice routes, but neither side gained a decisive upper hand. Trade caravans still crossed through Ottoman territory, yet new Atlantic routes diverted wealth and influence away from the traditional Silk Road pathways.

6. INTELLECTUAL AND CULTURAL LIFE

Despite the turmoil, the 17th century was not a cultural vacuum. Scholars continued to produce works on theology, history, geography, and mathematics. Sufi orders thrived in urban and rural settings, offering spiritual networks that sometimes acted as mediators between state authorities and local populations.

- **Evliya Çelebi** (1611–1682?), a famed Ottoman traveler, wrote an extensive travelogue called the **Seyahatnâme**, detailing his journeys across the empire and beyond. His accounts provide a rich tapestry of everyday life, architecture, customs, and folklore.
- Court-sponsored calligraphers and miniature painters created manuscripts depicting royal ceremonies, warfare, and religious festivals. These works, while not as grand as under Süleyman, still reflect the empire's continuing patronage of the arts.

7. THE QUESTION OF "DECLINE"

Traditional Decline Thesis

For centuries, historians attributed the empire's 17th-century difficulties to a moral and institutional decline following the "golden age" of Süleyman the Magnificent. They pointed to incompetent sultans, harem interference, corruption, and a failure to keep pace with European military advancements. From this perspective, the empire's internal fracturing appeared almost inevitable, a linear fall from past glory.

Revisionist Interpretations

Contemporary scholars argue that the 17th-century empire was undergoing a **"transformation"** rather than a uniform decline. They note that:

1. **Institutional Adaptation**: New forms of tax farming, a more prominent role for palace factions, and shifting recruitment strategies for the army signaled adjustments to evolving socio-economic conditions.
2. **Resilient State Structures**: Despite constant warfare, the empire survived repeated crises, brokered treaties, and maintained core territories.
3. **Continued Cultural Vibrancy**: Architecture, literature, and scholarship continued to flourish, indicating that the empire's cultural vitality was not extinguished.
4. **Global Context**: Many early modern states struggled with inflation, religious conflict, and administrative reorganization. The Ottomans were not alone in facing these challenges.

Therefore, while it is fair to discuss **relative** decline in military technology or administrative efficiency compared to earlier periods, painting the 17th century as a simple downfall overlooks the empire's adaptability and ongoing strengths.

8. KEY RULERS IN THE MID-TO-LATE 17TH CENTURY

Ibrahim I (1640–1648): Unrest and Downfall

Nicknamed "Ibrahim the Mad," Ibrahim I's reign was marked by erratic behavior and palace intrigues. While some accounts may exaggerate his eccentricities, it is clear that court factions maneuvered around him for power. Heavy taxation and lavish spending alienated various groups. His eventual deposition by the Janissaries reflected the ongoing tension between the palace and the military elite.

Mehmed IV (1648–1687) and the Emergence of the Köprülüs

Mehmed IV came to the throne as a child. The empire faced financial disarray, military setbacks, and rebellious provinces. This context paved the way for the **Köprülü family** of grand viziers who rose to prominence in the latter half of the 17th century, initiating reforms and temporarily revitalizing the empire. Their story will be central in the next chapter, illustrating how strong-willed viziers tried to restore Ottoman might.

9. PERSISTENT INTERNAL REVOLTS AND REBELLIONS

Celali Revolts in Anatolia

Throughout the century, the Celali movements flared repeatedly. While not uniformly ideological, they reflected broader discontent with corruption, heavy taxes, and the weakening of traditional land grants. Some leaders claimed to champion justice, attracting large followings of peasants and disaffected sipahis.

The state's response varied: sometimes harsh military suppression, sometimes negotiations and offers of amnesty. While the revolts never toppled the central government, they drained resources and disrupted agriculture in the Anatolian heartland.

Provincial Autonomy and Semi-Independent Rulers

Beyond Anatolia, local notables in the Balkans, the Arab provinces, and North Africa often operated with considerable autonomy. The state relied on them to maintain order and collect taxes, but in return, these notables expected freedoms that bordered on independence. This arrangement could be efficient in stable times but posed a risk if local rulers decided to challenge or ignore directives from Istanbul.

CHAPTER 14

KÖPRÜLÜ ERA AND ATTEMPTS AT REVIVAL

By the mid-17th century, the Ottoman Empire was embroiled in internal crises and external conflicts, prompting a new style of leadership to emerge from within the highest ranks of government. The **Köprülü family** of grand viziers rose to prominence, infusing the state with a burst of reformist energy and militant assertiveness. Beginning with **Köprülü Mehmed Pasha** in 1656, a succession of Köprülü-appointed or related viziers dominated Ottoman governance for several decades. They sought to restore central authority, crush rebellions, and reassert the empire's influence on the battlefield—especially in Hungary. This chapter explores the key figures of the Köprülü era, their ambitious reforms, military campaigns, and the lasting impact of their policies on Ottoman stability and power.

1. SETTING THE STAGE: MEHMED IV AND A CRISIS-RIDDEN EMPIRE

A Young Sultan Amidst Turmoil

When **Sultan Mehmed IV** took the throne in 1648, he was a child of about seven years old. Factionalism at court, severe financial strain, and ongoing military setbacks defined his early reign. Powerful harem figures and corrupt officials vied for influence, while the Janissaries remained a constant threat if their demands were not met. Provincial revolts, especially in Anatolia, continued to sap state resources.

The Turning Point of 1656

The situation deteriorated further until, in 1656, the Ottomans suffered a naval defeat at the **Battle of the Dardanelles** against Venetian forces. Panic gripped Istanbul as the Venetian blockade threatened the imperial capital's supplies. In desperation, key palace officials sought a strong and uncorrupt figure to restore order. They offered the position of grand vizier to **Köprülü Mehmed Pasha**, an experienced statesman reputed for integrity and firmness.

2. KÖPRÜLÜ MEHMED PASHA (1656–1661): RESTORING AUTHORITY

Conditions for Appointment

Köprülü Mehmed Pasha agreed to become grand vizier only if certain conditions were met:

1. He would have full authority to choose and dismiss high-ranking officials without palace interference.
2. No one, including the sultan's relatives or court favorites, would undermine his decisions.
3. He could enact wide-ranging reforms and punish corruption ruthlessly.

Surprisingly, the sultan and the palace elite accepted these demands. This gave Köprülü unprecedented power to enforce reforms—a scenario rarely seen in earlier decades when viziers struggled with competing palace factions.

Reforms and Centralization

Once in office, Köprülü Mehmed Pasha swiftly purged corrupt officials, reorganized the treasury, and cracked down on rebellious notables. He reasserted the state's monopoly on tax collection, reducing the influence of middlemen who exploited the peasantry. These measures brought immediate improvements in revenue and discipline.

He also tackled the Venetian threat in the Aegean, revitalizing the navy and fortifying the Dardanelles. While the Venetians still held Crete, Ottoman success in the naval sphere restored confidence in Istanbul. Köprülü Mehmed's strict governance style, while feared, effectively stabilized the empire's bureaucratic machinery during a dangerous period.

Personal Style

Köprülü Mehmed was known for his uncompromising stance. He did not hesitate to execute officials of high rank if they were found guilty of embezzlement or conspiracy. This zero-tolerance approach instilled a sense of order, though it also bred resentment and fear among the ruling elite. Yet, for the moment, this strategy worked: the empire began to recover from its worst administrative paralysis.

3. KÖPRÜLÜ FAZIL AHMET PASHA (1661–1676): EXPANSION IN HUNGARY

Succession of Power

Upon Köprülü Mehmed Pasha's death in 1661, the role of grand vizier passed to his son, **Köprülü Fazıl Ahmet Pasha**. Educated in religious law and statecraft, Fazıl Ahmet continued his father's policies with a somewhat less brutal style but equally strong determination. His appointment solidified the Köprülü family's hold on power and extended their reform agenda.

Military Focus: The Austro-Ottoman Wars

Fazıl Ahmet targeted Hungary, where Habsburg influence had grown. He personally led Ottoman campaigns to reassert control over Transylvania and the broader Danube region. In 1663–1664, the Ottomans faced the Habsburgs and allied forces in a series of battles. Though the famous **Battle of St. Gotthard** (1664) on the River Raab was a setback for Ottoman forces, they managed to negotiate a relatively favorable **Peace of Vasvár** (1664), retaining most of their conquests in Hungary. This deal, though controversial in Vienna, provided a decade of calm on the Habsburg front.

Conquest of Crete (1669)

Meanwhile, Fazıl Ahmet's leadership also oversaw the final capture of **Crete** from Venice in 1669, concluding a protracted siege of **Candia** (Heraklion). The war on Crete had lasted nearly a quarter of a century, draining Ottoman resources, but the ultimate victory affirmed the empire's naval and military capabilities. Gaining Crete secured maritime routes in the eastern Mediterranean and signaled Ottoman persistence in removing Venetian strongholds.

Domestic Policies and Patronage

While continuing the anti-corruption stance, Fazıl Ahmet also patronized scholarly and religious institutions. He helped fund the construction and maintenance of mosques, madrasas, and caravanserais. These projects aimed to unify populations under Ottoman oversight and facilitate trade and travel across the empire. His comparatively gentle approach (relative to his father's severity) won him some popularity, although the empire's strict centralization measures still sparked regional discontent in certain provinces.

4. MERZIFONLU KARA MUSTAFA PASHA (1676–1683): THE PUSH TOWARD VIENNA

Transition of Power

After Fazıl Ahmet's death in 1676, power shifted to **Merzifonlu Kara Mustafa Pasha**, another Köprülü protégé. Though not a blood relative of the Köprülü family, Kara Mustafa was closely allied with them, carrying on their legacy of strong centralized governance. He maintained good relations with Sultan Mehmed IV, who trusted him with the empire's grand strategies.

Renewed Ambitions in Europe

Kara Mustafa Pasha harbored grand designs to expand Ottoman power deeper into central Europe. Spotting weakness in the Habsburg realm—partly due to conflicts with France and internal strife—he advanced through Hungary in the early 1680s. By 1683, Ottoman forces, bolstered by contingents from vassal states, marched up the Danube with the ambitious goal of **besieging Vienna** once again.

The Second Siege of Vienna (1683)

Launched in July 1683, the Ottoman siege force encircled the city. Kara Mustafa hoped a swift victory would secure control over central Europe, possibly forcing the Habsburgs to accept vassalage. However, the siege dragged on. Ottoman leadership disagreements, insufficient siege artillery, and the defenders' resilience gave the Habsburgs time to organize a relief army. On September 12, 1683, a coalition led by Polish King **John III Sobieski** routed the Ottoman forces at the **Battle of Kahlenberg**, breaking the siege and forcing a chaotic Ottoman retreat.

Aftermath and Execution

The defeat at Vienna was catastrophic for Ottoman prestige. Kara Mustafa Pasha's failure triggered outrage in Istanbul. Blamed for overreaching and poor tactical decisions, he was executed by royal decree in Belgrade on December 25, 1683. The disastrous outcome ended the era of decisive Ottoman offensives in Europe, prompting a shift in regional power balances. The retreat from Vienna marked the start of a prolonged conflict known as the **Great Turkish War** (1683–1699), in which European coalitions would push the Ottomans back in several fronts.

5. ATTEMPTS TO REVITALIZE THE EMPIRE: MILITARY AND ADMINISTRATIVE ADJUSTMENTS

Post-Vienna Reforms

In the immediate wake of the Vienna defeat, the Ottoman court scrambled to regroup. Military reforms included modernizing artillery units, hiring foreign experts, and improving the Janissaries' discipline. Although some changes did occur, vested interests in the Janissary corps and among provincial notables limited how far these reforms could go.

Administratively, the central government sought to reaffirm control over tax collection, hoping to replenish the treasury depleted by years of war. Efforts were made to reduce the influence of tax farmers who exploited peasants, though these measures rarely succeeded in the long term without consistent enforcement.

The Role of Sultan Mehmed IV

Mehmed IV, who reigned until 1687, became increasingly unpopular after the Vienna debacle. Previously, he enjoyed success under the Köprülüs' guidance, but the humiliating defeat cast doubt on his leadership. Another palace faction emerged, culminating in Mehmed IV's deposition in 1687. He was replaced by his brother, **Suleiman II** (1687–1691), signaling the empire's desire for new direction in the face of European advances.

6. KÖPRÜLÜ LEGACY: GAINS AND LIMITATIONS

Temporary Revival of the Empire's Fortunes

The Köprülü family's ascendancy did much to stabilize the empire in the mid-17th century. Grand Viziers like Mehmed and Fazıl Ahmet reasserted central authority, cleansed the bureaucracy of some corrupt elements, and achieved notable military victories (e.g., Crete's conquest and Hungarian campaigns). For roughly three decades, they forestalled the worst consequences of factional strife, providing a semblance of unity and confidence.

Overreach and Setbacks

However, the drive to secure Vienna in 1683 proved a bridge too far. Kara Mustafa Pasha's ambition outstripped the empire's logistical capabilities and underappreciated European resilience. The catastrophic defeat initiated the empire's prolonged military retreat in Europe. While the Köprülü era revitalized state institutions, it did not resolve the underlying economic and social challenges (inflation, tax farming abuses, Janissary autonomy) that continued to simmer. Once faced with a robust European counteroffensive, the Ottomans struggled to maintain their forward positions.

Long-Term Influence

The Köprülü model of strong grand vizier authority—enforcing reforms from the top down—would inspire future attempts at centralized reform in the empire. The concept of an empowered vizier bypassing palace factions and making sweeping changes survived as an ideal even after the Köprülüs themselves were gone. Yet such centralized power also risked alienating entrenched interest groups, leading to violent backlashes or assassinations.

7. CONTINUING THE GREAT TURKISH WAR (1683–1699)

European Coalitions

Following the siege of Vienna, a "Holy League" formed—comprising Austria, Poland, Venice, and later Russia. This alliance aimed to drive the Ottomans out of Europe and reclaim territories lost over previous centuries. Ottoman defeats in battles across Hungary and the Balkans forced them to cede strategic forts and towns. The war spilled into multiple theaters, stretching Ottoman resources thin.

Internal Repercussions

Military losses fueled further discontent at home. Janissaries, facing grueling campaigns and dwindling pay, mutinied or deserted. Provincial revolts and brigandage rose. Administrators juggled war expenses with domestic relief efforts, but the economy remained under severe strain. The empire's diplomatic posture turned defensive, seeking peace deals to stave off deeper territorial erosion.

8. THE TREATY OF KARLOWITZ (1699)

Negotiating from a Position of Weakness

By the late 1690s, the Ottomans had lost control of most of Hungary and Transylvania. Exhausted by conflict and internal strife, the empire entered negotiations with the Holy League at **Karlowitz** (near modern-day Sremski Karlovci in Serbia). Signed in 1699, the **Treaty of Karlowitz** marked the first major territorial cession by the Ottomans in Europe:

- **Austria** gained significant parts of Hungary and Transylvania.
- **Venice** acquired territories in the Morea (southern Greece).
- **Poland** reclaimed Podolia from Ottoman control.

Although the treaty was humiliating for Ottoman pride, it reflected the new balance of power in southeastern Europe. For the first time, the empire recognized permanent territorial losses to European states, signifying a turn in Ottoman–European relations. Gone were the days of near-unstoppable Ottoman expansion into the heart of Europe. Instead, the empire entered the 18th century as a power forced to negotiate and adapt on more equal terms.

9. CONCLUSION OF CHAPTER 14

The Köprülü era demonstrated both the potential for revival and the limitations of top-down reform in the Ottoman Empire. Under a series of strong grand viziers, the state regained internal discipline, expanded in Crete, and held much of Hungary—at least temporarily. However, the disastrous siege of Vienna in 1683 and the ensuing defeats in the Great Turkish War showcased the empire's vulnerability when confronting a united European front. By the Treaty of Karlowitz (1699), the Ottomans officially ceded key territories, signaling a critical shift in European–Ottoman power dynamics.

Despite these setbacks, the empire was far from collapse. Ottoman institutions remained robust enough to recover from the losses, and new generations of officials and military leaders would continue to seek adaptations and reforms in the coming centuries. In the next chapter—**Chapter 15: The Long 18th Century and Shifting Global Powers**—we will examine how the Ottomans navigated a rapidly changing world, facing the rise of Russia, complex alliances with European states, and internal transformations that reshaped the empire's social and political fabric.

CHAPTER 15

THE LONG 18TH CENTURY AND SHIFTING GLOBAL POWERS

By the dawn of the **18th century**, the **Treaty of Karlowitz (1699)** had forced the Ottoman Empire to relinquish major European territories for the first time. This marked a critical turning point in Ottoman–European relations, as Austria, Venice, and Poland each gained lands at the empire's expense. While many observers at the time believed this signaled the empire's terminal decline, the reality was far more complex. The **18th century** (often called the "long 18th century" to include the later decades of the 17th century and the early decades of the 19th) saw the Ottomans adapt to new challenges and new alliances. They faced the rise of **Russia** as a formidable power, shifting commercial networks due to European maritime expansion, and internal administrative strains. Yet, the empire's flexibility and resilience enabled it to survive, reform, and even sporadically revive its fortunes. In this chapter, we delve into the state's evolving diplomatic strategies, economic reorientations, and social transformations that would shape the Ottomans' trajectory leading into the 19th century.

1. THE AFTERMATH OF KARLOWITZ AND THE EARLY 18TH CENTURY

Sultan Mustafa II and Ahmed III

Following the Treaty of Karlowitz, **Sultan Mustafa II (1695–1703)** attempted to restore Ottoman prestige through limited military campaigns and internal consolidation. However, continuing defeats and heavy taxes contributed to the 1703 rebellion known as the **Edirne Incident**, which led to Mustafa II's dethronement. In his place, the reform-minded **Ahmed III (1703–1730)** ascended the throne. Ahmed III's reign is often associated with a cultural and diplomatic renaissance—at least in certain circles of the capital—and is famously remembered for the **Tulip Era** in Istanbul, where European cultural influences and new forms of social life flowered among the elite.

The Shift Toward a Diplomatic Balance

Military defeat in the late 17th century taught the Ottomans the value of nuanced diplomacy. The empire realized it could no longer rely purely on martial superiority to handle European rivals. Instead, the Ottoman government increasingly employed **balance-of-power** tactics. Officials worked to exploit rivalries among European states—particularly between Austria, Russia, France, and Britain—to secure advantageous alliances or neutrality. Although the empire still engaged in warfare, it also invested more effort in negotiation and treaties, hoping to prevent a united European front against Ottoman interests.

2. THE RISE OF RUSSIA AND ITS IMPACT ON THE EMPIRE

Peter the Great and the Black Sea Frontier

A significant new challenger emerged on the **Black Sea frontier**: **Russia**, under the leadership of **Peter the Great (r. 1682–1725)**. Eager to access warm-water ports, Peter turned his gaze southward. The Ottomans had traditionally dominated the Black Sea coastline through alliances with the Crimean Khanate (a semi-autonomous vassal state). Now, Russian expansions into the north Black Sea plains threatened Ottoman control, culminating in conflicts like the **Pruth Campaign (1710–1711)**. In that war, the Russians marched toward the Danube principalities, only to be encircled by Ottoman and Crimean Tatar forces. Negotiations allowed Russia to withdraw, averting a total disaster for Peter. Nonetheless, the episode signaled the start of an enduring contest for influence in the Black Sea basin.

Later Russian Ambitions

After Peter's death, Russia continued to modernize and expand. Under rulers like **Catherine the Great (r. 1762–1796)**, Russian territorial ambitions encompassed parts of the Caucasus, the Crimean Peninsula, and the Danubian Principalities. The resulting wars between the Ottomans and Russia—fought intermittently through the 18th century—reshaped the strategic map of Eastern Europe and the Black Sea. Russian victories in battles and naval encounters, combined with diplomatic maneuvers, gradually eroded Ottoman hegemony in the region.

3. THE TULIP ERA (1718–1730) AND CULTURAL EXCHANGE

Peace and Prosperity?

A moment of relative peace arrived with the **Treaty of Passarowitz (1718)**, signed between the Ottomans, Austria, and Venice. This treaty ended the Ottoman–Venetian conflict over Crete and the Morea, while also stabilizing the Austrian frontier. In Istanbul, under the patronage of **Sultan Ahmed III** and his Grand Vizier **Nevşehirli Damat İbrahim Pasha**, the court indulged in a period of cultural flourishing and outward-looking reforms. Known in later historical memory as the **Tulip Era**, the empire embraced artistic, architectural, and intellectual influences from Europe.

- **Tulip Cultivation**: Aristocrats and wealthy bureaucrats displayed rare tulip bulbs—imported or selectively bred—as status symbols. Elegant garden parties and festivals became synonymous with the era's refined lifestyle.
- **Printing Press and Diplomatic Missions**: The first Ottoman Turkish printing press was established by **Ibrahim Müteferrika** (with partial impetus from earlier Jewish and Greek presses). At the same time, Ottoman delegations traveled to European capitals—especially Paris—absorbing ideas about military organization, fortifications, and even fashion and social customs.

Social Changes and Elite Consumption

While the capital's elite experimented with new fashions, coffeehouses, and literary salons, large sections of the population remained untouched by these cultural shifts. Indeed, some conservative factions criticized the lavish spending and perceived Westernization. They argued that the empire's spiritual and martial vigor was eroding. These social tensions would later contribute to a backlash against the regime.

4. THE PATRONA HALIL REVOLT (1730) AND END OF THE TULIP ERA

Causes of Discontent

Behind the glittering facade of the Tulip Era, economic strains and frustrations festered among soldiers, tradesmen, and religious conservatives. Renewed warfare against Persia (beginning in the late 1720s) placed additional burdens on the treasury. Meanwhile, rumors of extravagance at the court fueled resentment, especially among the Janissaries, who demanded better pay, and among merchants hurt by changing trade patterns.

The Outbreak of Revolt

In **1730**, a former sailor or mercenary named **Patrona Halil** led a group of discontented men—Janissaries, unemployed laborers, and others—on an uprising in Istanbul. They sacked homes and demanded an end to lavish expenditures, calling for the removal of the grand vizier. Sultan Ahmed III, caught off guard, sought to appease the rebels. He sacrificed his grand vizier, Nevşehirli Damat

İbrahim Pasha, and others close to the court. Eventually, the sultan himself was forced to abdicate, bringing the Tulip Era to a sudden and violent close.

Aftermath

The revolt underscored the precarious balance between the imperial court's ambitions for cultural and administrative reforms and the population's capacity for resistance. Ahmed III's successor, **Mahmud I (1730–1754)**, subdued the revolt and sought to restore order. While the immediate zeal for Western-influenced court culture was muted, the underlying necessity for modernization—particularly in military affairs—remained pressing.

5. MILITARY CONFLICTS AND REFORMS IN THE MID-18TH CENTURY

Wars with Persia and Russia

Throughout the mid-18th century, the Ottomans fought intermittent wars on multiple fronts:

1. **Persia (Safavid to Afsharid Transition)**: The Safavid dynasty collapsed internally, eventually replaced by **Nadir Shah** and the **Afsharid** dynasty. The Ottomans fought skirmishes in the Caucasus and Iraq regions, with each side alternately gaining or losing frontier territories.
2. **Russia**: After the Pruth Campaign, tensions remained high. Russia continued to push southward, culminating in the **Russo-Turkish Wars**

that erupted at various intervals. Each clash tested the Ottomans' ability to adapt militarily.

Emergence of Western-Style Military Reforms

Conscious of their repeated defeats, the Ottomans began introducing **Western-style military academies** and reorganizing select infantry and artillery units. French and other European military advisors were occasionally brought in to train Ottoman troops in modern drilling, fortification, and gunpowder weaponry. While these reforms faced opposition from conservative segments of the Janissary corps, some forward-thinking officials recognized that adopting European tactics and technology was essential for survival.

6. ECONOMIC SHIFTS AND GLOBAL TRADE

Declining Control Over Trade Routes

As European ships increasingly dominated global maritime commerce, the old Silk Road caravan routes through Ottoman territory lost some of their earlier value. While the empire remained a hub for regional markets—especially for Middle Eastern and Balkan goods—it struggled to benefit from overseas colonial wealth that flowed mostly into Western European ports.

Capitulations and European Merchants

Capitulations, commercial treaties granting favorable terms to European merchants, multiplied during the 18th century. These agreements offered tax exemptions and extraterritorial legal protections to foreign traders within Ottoman lands. While the empire initially viewed capitulations as a tool to encourage trade and leverage rivalries among European powers, over time, they empowered foreign merchants and chipped away at Ottoman economic sovereignty. French, British, and Dutch merchants established strong enclaves in major port cities like **Smyrna (Izmir)** and **Aleppo**, reaping significant profits often outside local jurisdiction.

Provincial Autonomy and Tax Farming

Internally, **tax farming** (iltizam) became even more common, as the central government sold the right to collect taxes in a certain district to private individuals. While this provided upfront revenue, tax farmers frequently squeezed peasants, fueling discontent. In some regions, powerful tax farmers (ayan) established de facto autonomous rule, challenging the central government's authority. The empire thus saw a gradual decentralization in certain provinces, paving the way for notable local dynasties or notables who would later negotiate power on their own terms.

7. PROVINCIAL RULERS AND REGIONAL DYNAMICS

The Rise of Local Strongmen

Across the vast empire, local notables, called **ayan** in Anatolia or various other titles in Arab provinces, emerged as power brokers. They negotiated with the central government, sometimes offering military assistance in exchange for recognition of their local autonomy. Notable examples include the **Mamluks in Iraq**, semi-independent pashas in North Africa, and strong families in the Balkans. While the Ottoman sultans technically remained overlords, their actual control over these regions varied, reflecting a looser structure that combined central bureaucracy with local fiefdoms.

Impact on Empire Cohesion

Such autonomy could stabilize provinces in the short term, reducing the burden on the central treasury. But in the long run, it eroded the empire's unitary nature. Provincial strongmen could ignore or defy imperial edicts if it suited their interests. Often, local populations saw these leaders as more immediate authorities than the distant sultan in Istanbul. This phenomenon foreshadowed the 19th century's shift toward more direct centralization efforts—efforts that would provoke conflicts between reformers and entrenched provincial elites.

8. THE ROLE OF WOMEN AND THE HAREM IN THE 18TH CENTURY

Continuity of the Valide Sultan Influence

Although the "Sultanate of Women" is more closely associated with the 17th century, mothers of the sultans (Valide Sultans) and other high-ranking women continued to exert political and social influence in the 18th century. They funded public works—mosques, fountains, schools—and often mediated disputes among court factions. Their patronage of artisans and scholars also shaped cultural life. However, with somewhat more stable sultans on the throne, the direct political power of the harem was more circumscribed compared to earlier eras.

Courtly Patronage and Charity

Elite women in the Ottoman court continued a long tradition of establishing charitable foundations (waqfs). These waqfs ranged from small soup kitchens to grand architectural complexes, reflecting both personal piety and a desire to assert social prestige. In times of crisis, such as after natural disasters or epidemics, these foundations offered essential relief to urban populations, sometimes enhancing the legitimacy of the dynasty and its supporting elites.

9. INTELLECTUAL AND CULTURAL LIFE IN THE 18TH CENTURY

Continued Literary and Artistic Output

Poetry, miniature painting, and calligraphy remained prestigious arts. Some poets infused their works with reflections on the empire's challenges, expressing both nostalgia for Süleiman's "golden age" and cautious optimism about new reforms. Translators rendered European scientific and philosophical texts into Ottoman Turkish, although such efforts were limited compared to the more extensive intellectual exchanges that would emerge in the 19th century.

Religious Scholarship and Sufi Orders

Sufi brotherhoods expanded in many regions, providing spiritual guidance and social cohesion. Orders like the **Naqshbandi** and **Mevlevi** had extensive networks from the Balkans to Arabia. Their lodges offered support to travelers, served as centers of local education, and sometimes influenced local politics. Meanwhile, the state retained a close relationship with the Sunni ulema (religious scholars), who controlled the legal courts and contributed to official ideological narratives. This interplay between mysticism, legal scholarship, and political authority was a hallmark of Ottoman cultural life.

10. THE LATER DECADES: WARS AND TREATIES

Russo-Turkish Conflicts Intensify

In the second half of the 18th century, conflicts with Russia became more frequent and disastrous for the Ottomans. Under **Catherine the Great**, Russia seized the Crimean Khanate (1783), effectively dismantling one of the Ottomans' key buffer states. The **Treaty of Küçük Kaynarca (1774)** ended one such war, granting Russia sweeping privileges, including the right to protect Orthodox Christians in the Ottoman domains—a precedent that would echo into future international disputes. Russia's new access to the Black Sea also allowed the creation of a Black Sea fleet, threatening the Ottomans' southern coastline.

War with Austria and the Balkan Question

Austria, sometimes allied with Russia, also pressed into the Balkans. The Ottomans lost additional territories in Serbia and other regions. Meanwhile, local Christian populations in the Balkans grew restless, influenced by

Enlightenment ideas and encouraged by foreign powers seeking to undermine Ottoman rule. Although large-scale Balkan uprisings were yet to come, these smaller revolts foreshadowed the empire's later 19th-century nationalist challenges.

Diplomatic Maneuvering and the French Connection

Balancing against Russia and Austria, the Ottomans sometimes found an ally in **France**, which had long-standing commercial ties via capitulations. French military advisors occasionally assisted in Ottoman naval and artillery reforms, while French diplomacy in Istanbul sought to counter Habsburg and Russian gains. However, the Franco-Ottoman alliance was not ironclad; it shifted with Europe's evolving alliances, particularly after the French Revolution (1789) introduced new ideological dimensions to European politics.

11. ADMINISTRATIVE REFORMS AND THE SEEDS OF MODERNIZATION

Emergence of Reformist Pashas

As the 18th century progressed, certain Ottoman statesmen recognized the urgent need for comprehensive modernization. Figures like **Grand Vizier Halil Hamid Pasha (1782–1785)** attempted partial military reforms, reorganizing the Janissaries and introducing new artillery schools. These efforts often met resistance from entrenched interests—Janissaries, ulema, and provincial ayan—who feared losing privileges. Yet the seeds of a more centralized, modern state were planted during these years.

The New Order Concepts

The concept of a **"New Order"** (Nizam-ı Cedid) started to emerge, proposing Western-style drilling, uniforms, and discipline for select Ottoman regiments. While these regiments remained small, their establishment symbolized a shift. Officials realized that the empire's survival required adopting elements of European military science and administrative efficiency. This idea would become more fleshed out under **Selim III** (r. 1789–1807) and later under the **Tanzimat reforms** of the 19th century.

12. END-OF-CENTURY TURMOIL: THE FRENCH REVOLUTION AND NAPOLEON

French Invasion of Egypt (1798–1801)

The 1790s brought the **French Revolution**, which dramatically altered Europe's political landscape. In a bold move, **Napoleon Bonaparte** invaded **Egypt** (an Ottoman province) in 1798, intending to disrupt British trade routes and expand French influence. The Ottomans, aligned with Britain and Russia against France, struggled to expel the invaders. Eventually, British naval power and local Ottoman forces forced the French withdrawal, but the event exposed the empire's vulnerability—its provinces could be attacked by a European power with relative ease.

The Legacy of the Egyptian Expedition

Although the French occupation of Egypt was short-lived, it left a profound impact. It opened the door for European "orientalist" scholarship (the Description de l'Égypte project) and modern administrative ideas, which some local Egyptian elites absorbed. The invasion also highlighted weaknesses in the Ottoman command structure. Recognizing these failings, the empire's leadership grew more determined to launch robust reforms in the 19th century to protect key provinces from foreign encroachment.

13. CONCLUSION OF CHAPTER 15

The **18th century** was a time of both attrition and adaptation for the Ottoman Empire. While the Treaties of Karlowitz and Passarowitz confirmed significant territorial losses, the empire was not a static entity in terminal decline. Instead, it deployed new diplomatic strategies, engaged in partial military reforms, and navigated an increasingly complex global economy. Externally, Russia emerged as the most formidable threat, systematically eroding Ottoman power in the Black Sea region, while Austria also remained a critical adversary in the Balkans. Internally, powerful local notables (ayan), the Janissaries, and entrenched bureaucratic elites resisted or shaped reforms, creating a multifaceted struggle over the empire's future trajectory.

Despite enduring defeats, the Ottomans displayed resilience, forging alliances and adopting selective Western military techniques. The seeds of a more comprehensive reform movement were planted, driven by leaders who recognized that maintaining a vast empire required embracing change. As the century drew to a close, the shock of the French invasion of Egypt underscored just how vulnerable Ottoman territories could be in an era of aggressive European expansion.

In the next chapter—**Chapter 16: The Era of Reforms (Tanzimat and Early 19th Century)**—we will explore how the empire moved from sporadic modernization efforts to a more systematic and wide-ranging program of reforms, particularly under sultans like **Mahmud II** and the architects of the **Tanzimat**. The 19th century would prove decisive in determining whether the Ottoman state could transform itself enough to survive in a world dominated by European imperial powers and rising national movements within its own borders.

CHAPTER 16

THE ERA OF REFORMS (TANZIMAT AND EARLY 19TH CENTURY)

By the early **19th century**, the **Ottoman Empire** was under immense pressure from multiple directions. Externally, rising European powers—especially Russia, Austria, Britain, and France—sought territorial or commercial advantages. Internally, the empire faced local rebellions, entrenched elites, and growing unrest among non-Muslim populations inspired by nationalism or seeking equal rights. In response, a series of sultans and reform-minded statesmen initiated broad overhauls of the state's military, administrative, and social structures. These efforts were collectively known as the **Tanzimat** (meaning "Reorganization"), although some important changes predated the official Tanzimat proclamations. From **Mahmud II's** centralizing policies to the promulgation of **Gülhane Hatt-ı Şerif** in 1839, the early 19th century witnessed profound transformations in how the empire governed and interacted with its diverse populations. This chapter explores these tumultuous decades, examining the motivations behind reform, the key figures driving change, and the obstacles that both slowed and shaped the reformist agenda.

1. THE PRELUDE TO MAHMUD II'S ERA

End of the 18th Century and the Impact of Napoleon's Invasion

As discussed in the previous chapter, **Napoleon Bonaparte's** invasion of Egypt (1798) exposed the empire's military vulnerability and foreshadowed the European appetite for colonial expansion in Ottoman territories. The invasion's aftermath galvanized some Ottoman officials, who saw the need for a modernized army and more direct central authority to withstand foreign threats. However, entrenched groups—including **Janissaries**, **provincial ayan**, and certain ulema—remained skeptical or hostile to adopting European-style reforms.

Selim III's Initial Reforms (Nizam-ı Cedid)

Before **Mahmud II**, **Sultan Selim III (r. 1789–1807)** sought to modernize the army under the banner of **Nizam-ı Cedid** ("New Order"). He created new infantry units trained and equipped in European fashion, reformed some financial practices, and opened permanent embassies in major European capitals. Although limited in scope, these moves signaled an important paradigm shift. However, the Janissaries and conservative ulema viewed the new regiments as a threat to their privileges and revolted in 1807, deposing Selim III. The short-lived reign of **Mustafa IV** (1807–1808) followed, culminating in violence and political upheaval.

2. MAHMUD II'S ASCENDANCE AND EARLY STRUGGLES

The Complex Path to Power

Mahmud II (r. 1808–1839) narrowly escaped the Janissary purges that ended Selim III's reign. He rose to the throne with the support of reformist notables who believed that only a strong sultan, committed to systematic modernization, could save the empire from disintegration. In his early years, Mahmud carefully navigated palace factions and the powerful Janissaries, avoiding open confrontation until he could consolidate enough support for decisive action.

Dealings with Provincial Notables (Ayan)

One of Mahmud's initial challenges was managing autonomous provincial leaders, especially in the Balkans and Anatolia. Figures like **Ali Pasha of Ioannina** in Greece and **Muhammad Ali** in Egypt operated almost as semi-independent rulers. Mahmud negotiated with them, sometimes granting titles or privileges, but he also prepared to assert central authority when an opportunity arose. This balancing act set the stage for future conflicts, notably the rising star of Muhammad Ali and his ambitions in the Levant.

3. THE DESTRUCTION OF THE JANISSARIES (1826)

Rising Tensions

By the 1820s, Mahmud II recognized that genuine reform required dismantling the **Janissaries**, who had stifled every attempt at creating a modern army. However, the Janissaries remained a potent force, not just militarily but also socially, as they had become embedded in urban trades and guilds. Sultan Mahmud spent years recruiting loyal officers and establishing small, modernized contingents quietly, learning from Selim III's mistakes.

The Auspicious Incident (Vaka-i Hayriye)

In **1826**, tensions reached a breaking point. Mahmud II announced the formation of a new Western-trained army corps, prompting Janissary riots in Istanbul. Seizing the moment, Mahmud ordered the loyal segments of the army and loyal city militias to suppress the revolt. The Janissary barracks were bombarded and many Janissaries were killed or arrested. This event became known as the **Auspicious Incident**—in Ottoman historiography, it signified the empire's liberation from Janissary obstruction, though it also involved brutal repression. In the aftermath, the Janissary corps was dissolved, and their property confiscated. Mahmud II swiftly replaced them with new units trained along European lines, finally opening the door to deeper military reform.

4. MAHMUD II'S REFORM AGENDA

Administrative and Bureaucratic Reorganization

Having eliminated the Janissary threat, Mahmud II moved to centralize the state apparatus:

1. **Ministries**: He established Western-style ministries (for War, Finance, Foreign Affairs), reducing the power of traditional offices and creating a clearer hierarchy.
2. **Provincial Governors**: New regulations aimed to limit the autonomy of local pashas, standardize tax collection, and enforce direct communication between provinces and Istanbul.

3. **Postal and Translation Offices**: Mahmud introduced a faster courier system and translation bureaus to handle European languages, vital for diplomatic and commercial relations.

Western-Style Institutions

Mahmud II was deeply influenced by European practices:

- He encouraged officials to adopt **Western dress** (the fez became mandatory in place of the Janissary turban).
- He sent students abroad to study military science, engineering, and medicine.
- He patronized newspapers and periodicals, though censorship was common.

These shifts were controversial among conservative factions. Nonetheless, the sultan believed that adopting European techniques was the only way for the empire to resist foreign encroachments and maintain internal order.

5. EXTERNAL PRESSURES AND LOST TERRITORIES

Greek War of Independence (1821–1830)

While Mahmud II was restructuring the empire, a major crisis erupted in the Balkans: the **Greek War of Independence** (1821). Greek revolutionary groups—backed by sympathetic European public opinion—rose up against Ottoman rule. Early Ottoman attempts to crush the revolt were brutal but not fully effective. Alarmed by the Ottoman approach, European powers (Britain, France, Russia) intervened, culminating in the **Battle of Navarino** (1827), where the Ottoman-Egyptian fleet was destroyed by allied navies.

Weakened on multiple fronts, the Ottomans had to accept Greek independence in 1830 under the **London Protocol**. The loss of Greece marked a symbolic blow, as it was the first major Christian territory in the Balkans to break away from Ottoman control since the 15th century.

Muhammad Ali's Ambitions in Egypt

Simultaneously, **Muhammad Ali** in Egypt sought to expand his domain, capturing parts of the Levant (Syria, Palestine) and threatening Ottoman authority.

Mahmud II appealed to European powers for support, fearful that Egypt's modernized forces could march on Istanbul. Eventually, a deal brokered by European diplomats forced Muhammad Ali to withdraw from Anatolia, but the crisis demonstrated the fragility of central Ottoman authority over key provinces.

6. THE ROAD TOWARD TANZIMAT: GÜLHANE HATT-İ ŞERİF (1839)

Mahmud II's Final Years and Legacy

By the 1830s, Mahmud II's health was failing. He had laid the groundwork for structural reforms, weakening conservative strongholds and consolidating a more centralized state. When he died in 1839, his successor, **Abdülmecid I**, inherited an empire in the midst of transformation, battered by regional crises but armed with new institutions. Mahmud's final legacy included a modernizing army and a bureaucracy more open to European administrative methods.

The Gülhane Edict

Shortly after Mahmud's death, a landmark proclamation—**Gülhane Hatt-ı Şerif (1839)**—was issued in the name of Abdülmecid I. Drafted with the assistance of reformist statesmen like **Mustafa Reşid Pasha**, the edict pledged:

1. **Security of Life, Honor, and Property** for all Ottoman subjects.
2. Fair and consistent taxation, reducing abuses by local officials.
3. A fair military conscription process and a limit on arbitrary punishments.

This edict is widely viewed as the formal starting point of the **Tanzimat** era—though many reforms traced back to Mahmud II and earlier efforts. Significantly, it implied a commitment to legal equality across religious lines, at least in principle, hinting at the empire's pivot toward a more inclusive civic notion of Ottoman citizenship.

7. EARLY TANZIMAT REFORMS AND REACTIONS

Implementation Challenges

While the Gülhane Edict promised sweeping changes, local realities complicated enforcement. Provincial governors sometimes resisted changes that limited their autonomy. Religious leaders questioned reforms that placed non-Muslims on a more equal legal footing. Additionally, the empire's financial strains remained acute. Funding modern schools, a standing army, and administrative salaries required new revenue sources and external loans, creating debt that would later weigh heavily on the Ottoman treasury.

Continued European Influence

European ambassadors and consuls closely monitored the reforms, pushing the Ottomans to accelerate measures that aligned with European conceptions of "civilization" and "progress." At the same time, these powers used the Ottomans' reform commitments to justify deeper intervention in the empire's internal affairs. For instance, France or Russia might demand protections for specific Christian communities, while Britain lobbied for expanded trade privileges and an end to slavery in certain Ottoman provinces.

8. SOCIETAL AND CULTURAL IMPACT

Emergence of New Elites

Mahmud II's reforms and early Tanzimat policies fostered the growth of a **Westernized Ottoman elite**—military officers, bureaucrats, translators, and merchants who had studied in European schools or served in embassies. They brought back ideas about constitutional government, legal codification, and cultural modernity. Over time, these elites formed the backbone of a nascent civil service class that championed further modernization.

Shift in Urban Life

Urban centers like **Istanbul, Izmir, Beirut**, and **Aleppo** saw the rise of modern educational institutions, printing presses, and newspapers—though under strict supervision. Modern theaters, Western-style clothing, and new forms of entertainment began to appear, at least among upper-class families. Social clubs and salons, occasionally mixing foreigners with Ottoman intellectuals, laid the groundwork for broader debates about national identity, governance, and the empire's future direction.

9. KEY PERSONALITIES IN EARLY 19TH-CENTURY REFORM

- **Mahmud II (r. 1808–1839)**: Led the charge in centralizing the empire, destroying the Janissaries, and establishing foundational administrative reforms.
- **Mustafa Reşid Pasha (1800–1858)**: A leading architect of the Gülhane Edict and an influential statesman who navigated European diplomatic circles.
- **Hüsrev Pasha**: Served under Mahmud II, aiding in military modernization and administrative restructuring.
- **Muhammad Ali of Egypt**: Though technically a vassal, he reformed Egypt's army and economy, challenging Istanbul's authority and showcasing an alternative model of modernization.

10. EXTERNAL CONFLICTS AND THE REFORMIST MOMENTUM

Continued Tensions with Muhammad Ali

During Abdülmecid I's reign, Muhammad Ali's ambitions in Syria provoked another crisis. European powers intervened to support the Ottoman government, resulting in the **Convention of London (1840)**, which compelled Muhammad Ali to withdraw from Greater Syria, though he kept hereditary rule in Egypt. The empire's reliance on European help reinforced the sultan's belief that internal consolidation and modernization were crucial for maintaining sovereignty.

European Wars and Diplomacy

As the 19th century advanced, the Ottomans found themselves caught in European power struggles. The empire's strategic position—controlling access from the Mediterranean to the Black Sea—made it a focus of the **"Eastern Question,"** in which European states debated how to manage or partition Ottoman territories without upsetting the balance of power.

11. BEYOND 1839: TOWARD A FULLER TANZIMAT AGENDA

Edict of 1856 and Further Reforms

The Gülhane Hatt-ı Şerif was only the beginning. The **Hatt-ı Hümayun of 1856** expanded on its provisions, promising full equality for Muslims and non-Muslims in law, education, and taxation. This progress, however, was both spurred and shaped by the **Crimean War (1853–1856)**, during which the empire allied with Britain and France against Russia. In return for Western support, the Ottomans agreed to more pronounced reforms, further opening the door to European influence.

Challenges to Full Implementation

Despite proclamations of equality, local power dynamics, religious traditions, and bureaucratic inertia slowed change. Christian and Jewish communities did gain some legal protections, yet discrimination and financial inequities persisted. Muslim conservatives lamented that the empire was abandoning Islamic precepts by adopting Western norms. Meanwhile, the economy remained fragile, and war expenses drove the Ottoman state into mounting debt, foreshadowing financial crises in the late 19th century.

12. CONCLUSION OF CHAPTER 16

The early 19th century was a watershed in Ottoman history, marked by the systematic drive to modernize and centralize state structures. **Mahmud II** initiated transformative policies—destroying the Janissaries, expanding the bureaucracy, adopting European military techniques—and laid the groundwork for the **Tanzimat**. The **Gülhane Edict (1839)** formalized many of these aspirations, announcing a new era of rights, administrative consistency, and legal reforms.

Yet, these reforms did not occur in a vacuum. They were deeply entangled with foreign pressures, local resistance, and the empire's ongoing financial burdens. The internal power struggles—between reformist bureaucrats and conservative factions, between Istanbul and regional authorities—continued to shape how effectively these changes took root. Moreover, European powers increasingly used the empire's reform promises as leverage to further their own strategic and economic interests.

In the coming chapter—**Chapter 17: Mahmud II, Abdülmecid I, and the Changing Face of the Empire**—we will delve more deeply into how these reforms impacted social structures, the relationship between the state and religious institutions, and the empire's global posture. We will also see the next wave of sultans and statesmen who attempted to carry the Tanzimat project forward, sometimes encountering fierce backlash and at other times achieving remarkable successes.

CHAPTER 17

MAHMUD II, ABDÜLMECID I, AND THE CHANGING FACE OF THE EMPIRE

In previous chapters, we explored the early 19th-century reforms that culminated in the abolition of the Janissary Corps and the dawn of the Tanzimat era. Yet, the broader transformation of the Ottoman Empire during this period goes beyond military reorganization. The reigns of **Mahmud II** (r. 1808–1839) and his successor **Abdülmecid I** (r. 1839–1861) reshaped nearly every facet of Ottoman life—from administration, taxation, and legal frameworks to cultural norms and social identities. These profound changes, spurred in part by European pressures and internal crises, signaled a decisive shift toward modern governance structures. Chapter 17 delves deeper into how Mahmud II's late reforms took root, how Abdülmecid I expanded upon them, and how these policy shifts altered the empire's political, social, and cultural landscape.

1. THE FINAL YEARS OF MAHMUD II: CONSOLIDATING REFORM

Centralizing Authority After 1826

After the **Auspicious Incident (1826)** ended Janissary opposition, Mahmud II focused on consolidating his reforms. Having neutralized the empire's most powerful conservative military element, the sultan now sought to rebuild state institutions. This included:

1. **New Military Corps**: Mahmud established modern regiments—often trained by European officers—to serve as the core of the Ottoman army.
2. **Reorganized Provincial Administration**: He replaced local power brokers (ayan) and rebellious governors with officials loyal to the center, though in practice, some strongmen retained autonomy in remote regions.
3. **Developing a Professional Bureaucracy**: Ministries for war, finance, foreign affairs, and internal administration emerged, each staffed by officials familiar with modern accounting, record-keeping, and sometimes European languages.

Expanding Diplomatic Engagement

As the empire's external conflicts multiplied—particularly the **Greek War of Independence (1821–1830)**—Mahmud II recognized the need for more skilled diplomats to negotiate with European powers. He sent young Ottomans to European capitals to study languages and observe diplomatic norms. Additionally, he elevated the status of the Ottoman translation bureaus and diplomatic departments, forging a new cadre of officials who combined Ottoman administrative traditions with familiarity in Western practices.

Cultural Markers of Reform

Mahmud II continued adopting Western habits to signal the empire's new direction. Court attire changed to simpler European-style uniforms adorned with the **fez**. The sultan also patronized newspapers, though they were limited in reach and subject to state oversight. Such symbolic gestures, while controversial among traditionalists, helped differentiate the new era from the empire's Janissary-dominated past.

2. ABDÜLMECID I ASCENDS THE THRONE (1839)

Succession and the Gülhane Edict

Upon Mahmud II's death in July 1839, his teenage son **Abdülmecid I** inherited a realm beset by problems: the Greek loss was a fresh scar, Muhammad Ali of Egypt posed a threat in the Levant, and European states were pressing for deeper reforms. Within months of Abdülmecid's accession, the empire issued the **Gülhane Hatt-ı Şerif** (1839), often cited as the formal start of the **Tanzimat** era. While the late Mahmud II had laid the groundwork, Abdülmecid I and his reformist ministers—like Mustafa Reşid Pasha—publicly committed to broad reorganization of administrative, legal, and social systems.

External Challenges and the Role of European Powers

Abdülmecid I's rule was immediately tested by ongoing disputes with **Muhammad Ali** in Egypt. European interventions (especially Britain and Austria) prevented a total Ottoman collapse, but these interventions came at a price: the empire was increasingly bound by European financial and diplomatic expectations. By aligning with Britain and Austria against Muhammad Ali, the Ottoman court also opened the door for further outside influence in its domestic affairs, including trade and legal standards.

3. THE SOCIAL IMPACT OF TANZIMAT REFORMS

Promises of Equality and Rights

One of the Tanzimat's most significant promises was the principle of **legal equality** for all Ottoman subjects, regardless of religion. The Gülhane Edict pledged to protect "life, honor, and property," and to reform taxation and conscription practices. This was a radical departure from the old system, where non-Muslims (dhimmis) paid a special poll tax (jizya) and faced various legal disadvantages.

Reception Among Religious Communities

- **Muslim Conservatives**: Some saw Tanzimat measures as eroding Islamic principles by placing Muslims and non-Muslims under the same legal framework.

- **Non-Muslim Communities**: Christians and Jews generally welcomed reforms that promised to remove old restrictions, but they remained cautious, aware that local officials or conservative neighbors might not fully respect new edicts.
- **Ulema's Stance**: The religious establishment, deeply entwined with the old system, was divided. Certain modern-minded clerics endorsed limited reforms, while others resisted changes that diminished their authority in legal matters.

Education, Press, and Intellectual Currents

State-sponsored schools began teaching European languages, sciences, and military disciplines. Private or missionary-run institutions also spread, introducing Western curricula to local elites. Newspapers and journals—some official, others semi-private—appeared, fostering debate on governance, culture, and social issues. This nascent "public sphere," especially in big cities, shaped how Ottomans perceived themselves and the empire's future.

4. THE CRIMEAN WAR (1853–1856) AND THE 1856 EDICT

Causes and Alliances

Abdülmecid I soon faced another major conflict: the **Crimean War**. Russia's ongoing expansion into the Black Sea region and claims to protect Orthodox Christians in the Ottoman domains triggered war in 1853. Fearing Russian dominance, Britain and France formed an alliance with the Ottomans. While the war was brutal, culminating in famous battles like **Sevastopol**, it also demonstrated the empire's new reliance on Western partners.

The Hatt-ı Hümayun (1856)

At war's end, the **Treaty of Paris (1856)** reaffirmed Ottoman sovereignty but obligated the empire to continue internal reforms. That same year, Abdülmecid I issued the **Hatt-ı Hümayun**, expanding on the Gülhane Edict's principles. It explicitly stated full equality of Muslims and non-Muslims in education, the military, and legal processes. This was designed partly to please Britain and France, who had championed the Ottoman cause against Russia. Yet it sparked controversy within the empire, prompting questions about how such equality would be implemented in practice, especially given centuries of entrenched social hierarchies.

Economic Consequences

The Crimean War inflicted heavy costs on the Ottoman treasury. To finance the conflict, the government took out **foreign loans** for the first time. This set a precedent for increasing reliance on European credit markets, which eventually led to severe debt crises in the latter 19th century. Moreover, the war's disruption to trade and agriculture exacerbated existing economic problems, fueling inflation and uneven development across different provinces.

5. DIPLOMATIC AND INTERNAL CHALLENGES DURING ABDÜLMECID I'S REIGN

Balancing Great Powers

Abdülmecid I and his ministers continuously negotiated with Britain, France, Austria, and other powers. On one hand, aligning with Western states offered the Ottomans military protection and financial aid. On the other, the sultan risked ceding too much autonomy, as foreign ambassadors often inserted themselves into local disputes—especially those involving Christian minorities.

Provincial Tensions

- **Balkans**: Growing nationalist sentiment among Serbs, Bulgarians, Romanians, and Greeks put pressure on Ottoman authorities. Uprisings or demands for autonomy periodically erupted, with local patriots citing Tanzimat promises to argue for greater political rights.

- **Arab Provinces**: In regions like Syria, Palestine, and Iraq, local notables navigated the new legal frameworks. Religious and communal leaders leveraged reforms to negotiate privileges, but underlying tensions between sectarian communities sometimes flared into violence.
- **Egypt**: Though nominally under Ottoman suzerainty, Egypt under Muhammad Ali's descendants maintained a separate path of modernization and relative autonomy, complicating Istanbul's efforts to project authority.

6. ECONOMIC AND ADMINISTRATIVE REORGANIZATION

Taxation and Revenue Reforms

The empire attempted to standardize taxation, abolishing older levies and feudal dues in favor of more direct revenue collection. However, corruption and resistance from entrenched local elites made implementation patchy. Many peasants found themselves caught between high official taxes and unofficial demands from local power holders.

Land Codes and Property Rights

In 1858, a new **Land Code** aimed to clarify property rights and encourage agricultural development. It allowed private ownership, but required registration—a process often manipulated by wealthier or better-connected individuals who registered land in their names, displacing traditional communal or family landholders. While some argue this code laid the foundations of a modern property regime, others note it also contributed to rural inequalities.

Growth of a Centralized Bureaucracy

Tanzimat reforms created a larger, more complex bureaucracy staffed by men educated in new schools, skilled in foreign languages and Western accounting methods. This class of civil servants, often called **bureaucratic reformers**, gained influence in the palace and the Sublime Porte (the Ottoman central government). Over time, they would push for further constitutional or administrative reforms, clashing with more conservative interests that favored traditional hierarchy and Islamic legal norms.

7. EDUCATION, THE PRESS, AND CULTURAL MODERNITY

Modern Education Initiatives

Building on Mahmud II's military academies, Abdülmecid I oversaw the proliferation of state-funded secondary schools (rüşdiye) and specialized institutions focusing on medicine, engineering, and administration. Meanwhile, mission schools and foreign-language schools offered alternative curricula, often introducing students to European literature, sciences, and political ideas. These parallel systems shaped an emerging middle class with cosmopolitan outlooks.

The Expanding Ottoman Press

Periodicals like **Takvim-i Vekayi** (the official gazette) and **Ceride-i Havadis** (semi-official newspaper) disseminated news and state decrees. Private newspapers—albeit censored—began critiquing local officials or discussing European ideologies. Intellectuals debated the empire's future, questioning whether Western-style constitutionalism, liberal economics, or Islamic-based revival held the best path forward. Istanbul, Beirut, and Izmir emerged as intellectual hubs where writers and reformers mingled in coffeehouses, literary salons, and reading clubs.

Shifting Urban Culture

The presence of European consuls and merchants, along with the new educational class, altered urban lifestyles. Western-style clothing became more common among officials; Western music, theater, and dances found small but devoted audiences in Istanbul's cosmopolitan districts like Pera (Beyoğlu). At the same time, tensions arose between old neighborhoods—adhering to more traditional norms—and newer enclaves that embraced modern amusements.

8. GROWING NATIONALISM IN THE BALKANS AND OTHER REGIONS

Emergence of National Movements

The Tanzimat's promises of equality inadvertently fueled nationalist sentiments among Balkan Christians who demanded not only equal rights but also political autonomy or independence. Bulgarian, Serbian, and Romanian intellectuals formed cultural societies, published newspapers in their native languages, and promoted national histories—efforts that eventually led to open revolts or international interventions.

Religious Reforms and Autocephalous Churches

One catalyst for Balkan nationalism was the movement to establish **autocephalous (independent) Orthodox churches**, free from the authority of the Greek-dominated Patriarchate of Constantinople. For instance, the **Bulgarian Exarchate** was recognized in 1870 after years of Bulgarian lobbying, reflecting how the Tanzimat environment allowed groups to press for religious-cultural autonomy. These developments weakened central Ottoman influence, as local communities viewed religious emancipation as a stepping stone to broader national aspirations.

9. THE LEGACY OF MAHMUD II AND ABDÜLMECID I

Achievements and Limitations

Under Mahmud II, the empire shed medieval military structures, embraced new administrative systems, and established a more centralized bureaucracy. Abdülmecid I carried these reforms forward, embedding them in formal edicts (Gülhane and Hatt-ı Hümayun) that reshaped law, social relations, and foreign policy alignments. Yet these reforms faced chronic obstacles:

1. **Financial Strain**: War debts and reliance on foreign loans burdened the state treasury.

2. **Regional Resistance**: Traditional elites, religious authorities, and local notables often undermined or selectively interpreted reforms.
3. **Nationalist Pressures**: Promises of legal equality fueled Balkan and other nationalist movements, leading to unrest and, eventually, new losses of territory.

A Bridge to Later Transformations

Still, the achievements of Mahmud II and Abdülmecid I were foundational. They created a cadre of reformist bureaucrats, modernized certain institutions, and introduced new concepts of citizenship and law. This legacy would inspire subsequent sultans and statesmen—like Abdülaziz, Abdülhamid II, and the Tanzimat architects—to push reforms even further, culminating in a constitutional experiment by the late 19th century.

10. CONCLUSION OF CHAPTER 17

Throughout the reigns of **Mahmud II** and **Abdülmecid I**, the Ottoman Empire underwent a dramatic metamorphosis. The Janissaries, once a symbol of Ottoman military might, were replaced by modern regiments. Central institutions took shape, informed by European administrative models. The Tanzimat reforms attempted to craft a legal framework in which all subjects, Muslim and non-Muslim alike, would share equal rights. Coupled with shifts in education, press freedoms, and evolving urban cultures, these developments constituted a watershed moment in Ottoman history.

However, these reforms did not uniformly succeed. Internal resistance, financial weaknesses, and nationalist movements plagued the empire, revealing the complexities of modernization in a multi-ethnic, multi-religious state navigating an era of aggressive European imperialism. Even so, the seeds of a modern Ottoman polity had been planted—seeds that would grow, clash, and transform further in the decades to come.

CHAPTER 18

CONTINUED REFORM EFFORTS AND INTERNAL STRUGGLES IN THE LATE 19TH CENTURY

Having established the groundwork of the Tanzimat during the reigns of Mahmud II and Abdülmecid I, the Ottoman Empire entered the **late 19th century** still committed to modernization yet beset by deepening dilemmas. **Abdülaziz (r. 1861–1876)** and **Abdülhamid II (r. 1876–1909)** grappled with a rapidly changing landscape: nationalist revolts in the Balkans, mounting foreign debt, and a shifting balance of power in Europe that often left the Ottomans isolated. Internally, the empire saw the emergence of a new generation of reformers—some calling for a constitutional monarchy and broader civil liberties, others favoring cautious centralization to maintain imperial unity. Chapter 18 delves into these competing reform efforts, examines the empire's struggle with financial crises, explores the rise of constitutional movements, and tracks how the Ottomans navigated the complex interplay of domestic and international pressures in the latter half of the 19th century.

1. THE REIGN OF SULTAN ABDÜLAZIZ (1861–1876)

Consolidating the Tanzimat Legacy

Upon **Abdülmecid I's** death, his brother **Abdülaziz** ascended to a throne still in flux. Early in his rule, he reaffirmed the Tanzimat principles. Reformist bureaucrats, such as **Ali Pasha** and **Fuad Pasha**, continued to spearhead administrative changes:

1. **Education**: The government supported new secondary schools and specialized academies (for military, engineering, and civil administration).
2. **Legal Codes**: Drawing on French civil and commercial laws, the Ottomans revised statutes to align with modern concepts of contract, property, and individual rights—though Sharia courts still handled personal status issues for Muslims.
3. **Provincial Reforms**: The **Vilayet Law (1864)** reorganized provinces into larger administrative units (vilayets), each with a governor, council, and a structured hierarchy to reduce corruption.

Financial Strains and Foreign Debt

However, the empire's ongoing military expenditures—particularly in attempts to quell Balkan unrest—and infrastructural projects (such as railways and telegraphs) demanded substantial capital. To fund these initiatives, Abdülaziz's government turned increasingly to European loans. By the late 1860s, debt repayment consumed a significant portion of the state budget, weakening Ottoman fiscal sovereignty and leading to eventual default.

Internal Opposition and Autocratic Tendencies

As debt and dissent grew, Abdülaziz became more authoritarian. He curtailed press freedoms and tightened censorship, fearing that liberal intellectuals and constitutional advocates might undermine his reign. This shift alienated many reformist elites who had once supported him. By the mid-1870s, widespread dissatisfaction with Abdülaziz's policies—exacerbated by new crises in the Balkans—led influential ministers and military officers to consider removing him from power.

2. NATIONALISM AND REVOLT IN THE BALKANS

The Balkan Powder Keg

The late 19th century saw **Bulgarians, Bosnians, Serbs, Montenegrins, Romanians**, and others pushing for greater autonomy or outright independence. Secret societies, church movements, and armed bands challenged Ottoman authority. The **Bulgarian Church's** struggle for independence from the Greek Patriarchate gained traction, sparking broader Bulgarian national consciousness. Elsewhere, Serbs and Montenegrins sought to expand territories at Ottoman expense.

The Eastern Crisis (1875–1878)

Revolts in **Bosnia** and **Herzegovina** (1875) and Bulgaria (1876) spiraled into an **Eastern Crisis**. European newspapers featured sensationalized reports of Ottoman atrocities, especially the **Bulgarian Horrors**, fueling anti-Ottoman sentiment in liberal Western circles. Russia, portraying itself as protector of Slavic Orthodox Christians, escalated diplomatic and military pressure, culminating in the **Russo-Turkish War (1877–1878)**. These events would drastically reshape the empire's European boundaries.

3. THE BRIEF REIGN OF MURAD V AND THE RISE OF ABDÜLHAMID II

Abdülaziz's Deposition (1876)

As unrest escalated, key Ottoman ministers and military leaders engineered a coup in 1876, deposing Abdülaziz. His nephew **Murad V** briefly replaced him. Reformist hopes soared, as Murad V was rumored to sympathize with constitutional ideals. Yet the new sultan's mental health issues, combined with the empire's external crises, made it impossible for him to consolidate power. Within months, he was deemed unfit to rule.

Abdülhamid II Takes the Throne (1876)

Abdülhamid II then ascended, inheriting a state on the brink of war with Russia. Initially, he appeared receptive to constitutionalists. Under pressure from reformists like **Midhat Pasha**, he approved the **First Ottoman Constitution (1876)**, establishing a bicameral legislature. However, the empire's dire circumstances and Abdülhamid's personal inclinations soon led to a different course, as we will see.

4. FINANCIAL COLLAPSE AND THE PUBLIC DEBT ADMINISTRATION

Declaring Bankruptcy (1875)

Even before the deposition of Abdülaziz, the empire had declared a partial moratorium on its debts in 1875. By then, revenues from agriculture and customs could not keep pace with interest obligations. European creditors demanded direct oversight of Ottoman finances to ensure loan repayments.

The Decree of Muharrem (1881)

Abdülhamid II faced reality in 1881 by issuing the **Decree of Muharrem**, establishing the **Ottoman Public Debt Administration (OPDA)**. This foreign-controlled body took over key revenue sources—like the salt monopoly and tobacco taxes—to guarantee debt service. Effectively, the OPDA functioned as a "state within a state," diminishing Ottoman fiscal independence. While it stabilized foreign investments, it fueled resentment among Ottoman patriots who saw the arrangement as yet another encroachment on sovereignty.

5. ABDÜLHAMID II'S AUTOCRATIC TURN AND THE SUSPENSION OF THE CONSTITUTION

The 1877–1878 Russo-Turkish War and Treaty of Berlin

Shortly after Abdülhamid II proclaimed the constitution in 1876, war with Russia commenced. The **Russo-Turkish War (1877–1878)** ended disastrously for the Ottomans, who signed the **Treaty of San Stefano**, conceding huge territories. Fearing Russian dominance, other European powers revised the treaty at the **Congress of Berlin (1878)**. While the Berlin settlement reduced Russian gains, it also recognized the independence of **Romania, Serbia, and Montenegro**, and granted autonomy to **Bulgaria**. Bosnia-Herzegovina was placed under Austrian occupation. These losses ignited debates on whether reforms had failed or were insufficient to maintain imperial integrity.

Suspending the Constitution

Citing the emergencies of war and territorial dismemberment, Abdülhamid II suspended the 1876 constitution in 1878 and dissolved the fledgling parliament. From then on, he ruled autocratically, concentrating power in the palace. While he maintained certain reformist measures in education and infrastructure, the sultan employed a vast spy network and censorship apparatus to silence dissent. This era came to be known as the **Hamidian regime**, marked by a combination of modernization drives and political repression.

6. EDUCATIONAL AND TECHNOLOGICAL MODERNIZATION UNDER ABDÜLHAMID II

Schools and Universities

Despite his autocratic rule, Abdülhamid II promoted significant educational reforms:

1. **Expansion of Rüşdiye**: State middle schools multiplied, teaching modern sciences and languages.
2. **Darülfünun** (University) Reorganization: Although the first Ottoman university had shaky beginnings, the sultan restructured and funded it, hoping to train loyal civil servants and professionals.

3. **Teacher Training**: New institutions prepared teachers in modern pedagogical methods, standardizing curricula across the empire.

Infrastructure and Communication

Abdülhamid II also invested in **railways**, telegraph lines, and roads to enhance central control. Projects like the **Anatolian Railway** and the **Hejaz Railway** improved military mobilization and facilitated pilgrimage routes to Mecca. Foreign companies often financed these ventures, intensifying foreign economic influence but also connecting distant provinces more closely to Istanbul.

7. THE RISE OF OPPOSITION: YOUNG OTTOMANS AND YOUNG TURKS

Intellectual Roots of the Opposition

Throughout Abdülhamid II's regime, a new generation of reform-minded intellectuals, officials, and army officers criticized the sultan's autocracy. Inspired by the earlier Tanzimat spirit and European liberal ideas, they argued that the empire needed a constitutional framework to unite its diverse peoples and address modern challenges. The **Young Ottomans** were among the earliest groups, blending Islamic principles with concepts of popular sovereignty, but they were largely suppressed.

Emergence of the Young Turks

By the 1880s and 1890s, younger dissidents—later labeled **Young Turks**—began organizing secret societies. Many lived in European exile, publishing newspapers that advocated for constitutional rule, the rule of law, and limitations on palace authority. The movement eventually coalesced under organizations like the **Committee of Union and Progress (CUP)**, which would gain significant traction in the early 20th century. Although not yet strong enough to topple Abdülhamid II, they laid the intellectual and organizational groundwork for future revolutions.

8. SOCIETAL SHIFTS AND COMMUNAL POLITICS

Pan-Islamism and Ottomanism

Facing a fracturing empire, Abdülhamid II promoted
Pan-Islamism—emphasizing the sultan's role as Caliph of all Muslims worldwide. This policy aimed to rally Muslim loyalty at home and in colonial territories

under European rule. Simultaneously, official rhetoric still invoked **Ottomanism**, the 19th-century ideal that all subjects, regardless of faith, could share a common loyalty to the empire. In practice, these two ideologies sometimes clashed, as Pan-Islamic sentiments alienated Christian populations who saw the state pivoting away from religious equality.

Armenian and Other Non-Muslim Communities

The late 19th century also witnessed heightened tensions with **Armenian** communities, particularly in eastern Anatolia. Armenian activists demanded reforms to curb abuses by local Kurdish tribal leaders and to gain more equitable taxation. Fearing separatism, the Hamidian regime responded with crackdowns, culminating in the **Hamidian Massacres (1894–1896)**, where thousands of Armenians perished. This violence drew international condemnation and intensified criticisms of Abdülhamid II's policies.

9. THE FINANCIAL AND ADMINISTRATIVE LEGACY

Debt Administration and Economic Dependencies

By the end of the 19th century, the **Ottoman Public Debt Administration** had become a permanent fixture, controlling a sizable share of imperial revenues. European banks financed key infrastructure while reaping profits and exercising leverage over Ottoman policy decisions. Local industries, such as textiles, struggled to compete with cheaper European imports, contributing to uneven economic development.

Reform Outcomes

Though the empire's political system returned to autocracy, many Tanzimat-era administrative structures—centralized ministries, standardized education, and revised legal codes—remained in effect. These institutions continued to evolve, sometimes under the watchful eye of foreign advisors or officials. In some provinces, local councils gave elites a taste of shared governance, fostering an awareness that the empire's governance was no longer a purely top-down affair.

CHAPTER 19

THE EARLY 20TH CENTURY, INTERNAL CHALLENGES, AND EXTERNAL PRESSURES

By the dawn of the **20th century**, the **Ottoman Empire** had spent decades attempting to modernize its institutions and resist foreign encroachment. Despite significant reforms under **Abdülmecid I**, **Abdülaziz**, and particularly **Abdülhamid II**, the empire remained beset by internal dissent, nationalist movements, and intense great-power rivalries that shaped its external relations. Emerging reformist factions—collectively referred to as the **Young Turks**—questioned the Hamidian autocracy and demanded a return to constitutional rule. Meanwhile, European powers continued to vie for influence within the empire's borders, often exacerbating local tensions. This chapter examines the empire's precarious situation in the early 1900s, the revolutions that brought constitutionalism back to the forefront, and the escalating international crises that set the stage for the empire's final, tumultuous decade.

1. THE LATE HAMIDIAN ERA AND RUMBLINGS OF CHANGE

Abdülhamid II's Consolidation and Repression

Following the **Russo-Turkish War (1877–1878)** and the **Treaty of Berlin**, Sultan **Abdülhamid II** (r. 1876–1909) suppressed the short-lived Ottoman constitution of

1876, ruling with tight centralized authority. His regime combined elements of modernization—railways, telegraphs, expanded education—with an extensive security apparatus. The palace spied on bureaucrats, exiled critics, and censored the press to prevent the spread of liberal or nationalist ideologies.

Despite these efforts, the empire's structural vulnerabilities remained. Financially, the **Ottoman Public Debt Administration** drained resources. Politically, non-Turkish populations in the Balkans and Arab provinces resented centralized rule. Intellectually, disillusioned students and officials formed underground networks calling for a revival of constitutional government. By the turn of the century, seeds of resistance had sprouted across the empire's diverse landscapes.

Young Turks and Secret Societies

Various dissident groups emerged, including the **Committee of Union and Progress (CUP)**, initially formed by medical students in Istanbul. Many members operated from exile in European cities like Paris or Geneva, publishing newspapers critical of the sultan and advocating for a return to the 1876 constitution. They argued that only constitutionalism, representative institutions, and transparency could hold the empire together amid rising nationalism.

In response to Hamidian censorship, these groups smuggled publications into Ottoman territory, rallying segments of the educated elite and the military. Young officers stationed in distant garrisons—frustrated by poor conditions and limited career prospects—became particularly receptive to CUP propaganda. Though still fragmented in the early 1900s, they would soon coalesce into a powerful movement.

2. THE MACEDONIAN PROBLEM AND BALKAN INSTABILITY

Unrest in Macedonia

No region illustrated Ottoman fragility in the early 20th century as starkly as **Macedonia**. A multi-ethnic province populated by Slavs, Greeks, Albanians, Turks, and Vlachs, it became the focus of competing nationalist claims. Bulgarian, Greek, and Serbian revolutionary committees vied for influence, sometimes resorting to guerrilla tactics. European powers—keen to protect

Christian minorities—demanded administrative reforms that infringed on Ottoman sovereignty.

Abdülhamid II dispatched new gendarmerie units, led partly by foreign officers, to restore order, but frequent skirmishes persisted. The resulting tension provided a rallying point for Young Turk activists, who viewed the empire's bungled handling of Macedonia as proof that the Hamidian regime was ineffective and internationally discredited.

Great Power Intervention

Austria-Hungary, Russia, and other European states exploited the Macedonian situation to extend their influence. Joint "reform programs" placed foreign officers in local police forces and mandated special tax arrangements, further eroding Ottoman autonomy. The sultan's government bristled at these incursions but lacked the leverage or unity to counter them effectively. Meanwhile, Balkan states supported insurgent bands, anticipating that international pressure would eventually force the empire to cede more territory.

3. THE YOUNG TURK REVOLUTION (1908)

Rising Discontent in the Military

By 1906–1907, conspiracies within the **Ottoman Third Army** in **Monastir (Bitola)** and **Salonika (Thessaloniki)** intensified. Junior officers who had come under

CUP influence believed that a constitutional order would restore military morale and secure the empire's boundaries against further Balkan encroachments. Convinced that Abdülhamid's autocracy was undermining the empire's survival, they prepared to act.

The 1908 Coup and Restoration of the Constitution

In July 1908, the Young Turk revolution began in Macedonia. Army units mutinied, refusing to obey Istanbul's orders. Proclaiming loyalty to the idea of the constitution, they demanded the reinstatement of the suspended 1876 framework. Faced with a potential civil war, Abdülhamid II capitulated, announcing the **restoration of the constitution** and summoning a new parliament. Overnight, the empire shifted from Hamidian absolutism to a constitutional monarchy—at least on paper.

This sudden transformation, often celebrated as the **Young Turk Revolution**, unleashed widespread euphoria, especially among educated elites and marginalized communities who believed that constitutionalism would guarantee rights and halt foreign domination. In Istanbul, people of different ethnic and religious backgrounds paraded in the streets, chanting slogans of **hürriyet** (liberty).

4. STRUGGLES WITHIN THE NEW CONSTITUTIONAL ORDER

The Countercoup of 1909

Despite initial optimism, the new regime faced immediate challenges. Conservative factions—composed of religious scholars, palace loyalists, and some commoners wary of rapid change—resented the CUP's secular leanings and abrupt power shift. In April 1909, a revolt in Istanbul, labeled the **31 March Incident**, attempted to restore Sultan Abdülhamid's absolute authority. For a moment, it seemed the constitutional experiment would collapse.

However, the **Action Army**, led by Mahmud Shevket Pasha and loyal to the CUP, marched from Macedonia to Istanbul, suppressing the revolt. They forced Abdülhamid II's abdication, replacing him with his more pliant brother, **Mehmed V**. Though the sultan's role became largely symbolic, this move cemented the CUP's grip on central power—albeit at the cost of deepening internal divisions.

Factionalism and the CUP

The CUP itself was hardly monolithic. Some members advocated liberal democratic reforms and decentralization, while others preferred a strong centralized state. Nationalist trends also grew within the CUP, emphasizing Turkish language and culture, which alienated non-Turkish communities expecting equal recognition. These tensions would later influence the empire's wartime policies and shape the emergent politics of the region.

5. TENSION IN THE BALKANS AND THE ITALO-TURKISH WAR (1911–1912)

Balkan Antagonisms and Pre-War Maneuvers

While the Ottomans struggled to stabilize the constitutional regime, Balkan states (Serbia, Greece, Bulgaria, and Montenegro) forged alliances, sensing Ottoman weakness. Their leaders saw a chance to expel the empire from its remaining European territories. The empire's attempts to placate these ambitions—through reforms in Macedonia—proved insufficient.

Italy's Seizure of Libya

Meanwhile, Italy, eager to join the scramble for colonial territories, targeted the Ottoman province of **Tripolitania** (modern Libya). In 1911, Italian forces invaded, beginning the **Italo-Turkish War**. The Ottomans, stretched thin, faced immense logistical difficulties defending a far-flung desert territory. Despite heroic resistance from Ottoman officers like **Mustafa Kemal (Atatürk)** and Enver Pasha, the empire eventually lost control of Libya. Italy also seized the Dodecanese

Islands in the Aegean. This humiliating defeat revealed the empire's strategic vulnerability and emboldened Balkan states to plan their own offensives.

6. THE BALKAN WARS (1912–1913)

The First Balkan War

In October 1912, the **Balkan League** (Serbia, Bulgaria, Greece, and Montenegro) launched a coordinated attack against Ottoman positions in Macedonia and Thrace. Ottoman forces, undermined by disorganization and the continuing fallout from internal power struggles, suffered rapid defeats. Within weeks, Bulgarian armies approached the outskirts of **Istanbul**, while the Greeks and Serbs claimed large swaths of territory in the south and west.

Faced with disaster, the empire sued for peace. The **Treaty of London (1913)** stripped the Ottomans of almost all their European holdings west of **Edirne**, save for a small zone around Istanbul. This outcome was a devastating blow, uprooting centuries of Ottoman presence in the Balkans and triggering a massive influx of Muslim refugees (muhacirs) into Anatolia.

The Second Balkan War

Tensions among the victorious Balkan allies soon erupted into the **Second Balkan War** (June–July 1913), primarily pitting Bulgaria against its former partners. The Ottomans seized the opportunity to reclaim **Edirne**, restoring a semblance of pride after the First Balkan War's humiliations. Still, the net outcome remained dire: the empire lost most of its remaining European provinces, intensifying nationalist sentiments among Turks and fueling a sense of existential crisis within the CUP-led government.

7. DOMESTIC REALIGNMENTS AND AUTHORITARIAN TRENDS

CUP Ascendancy

In the wake of successive defeats, the Committee of Union and Progress consolidated its power. Senior CUP leaders—Enver Pasha, Talat Pasha, and Cemal Pasha—formed a triumvirate that effectively directed state affairs. A parliament still existed, but debates were often overshadowed by the CUP's strong influence and the sense that urgent decisions were necessary to save the empire.

Internal Repressions and Policy Shifts

Growing xenophobia and nationalist impulses emerged, as many Ottomans blamed the empire's setbacks on foreign machinations or internal disloyalty. Non-Turkish communities—Arabs in particular—voiced complaints that the new constitutional authorities were more concerned with Turkish nationalism than genuine equality. The CUP responded with a mix of reforms and crackdowns, resulting in an increasingly authoritarian system ironically led by a group once known for championing constitutionalism.

8. EUROPEAN ENTANGLEMENTS: TOWARD THE GREAT WAR

Global Power Alignments

In the early 1910s, Europe was divided into two major alliances: the **Triple Entente** (Britain, France, Russia) and the **Triple Alliance** (Germany, Austria-Hungary, Italy). Seeking external support to stave off further territorial losses, the Ottoman leadership considered alliances with different powers. Germany, eager for influence in the Middle East and strategic routes to Asia, courted Ottoman goodwill by providing military advisors (notably **Liman von Sanders**).

The July Crisis (1914) and Ottoman Maneuvering

When the **Assassination of Archduke Franz Ferdinand** in Sarajevo (June 1914) triggered the **July Crisis**, the great powers spiraled toward general war. Ottoman diplomacy wavered. Some officials, skeptical of Russia, pushed for alignment with the Central Powers (Germany and Austria-Hungary). Others worried that siding against Britain and France—dominant naval powers—might be suicidal. Ultimately, secret negotiations led to an Ottoman-German alliance, sealed just before the outbreak of **World War I**.

9. WORLD WAR I AND THE OTTOMAN ENTRY (1914–1918)

The Decision to Join

In October 1914, Ottoman warships under German command bombarded Russian Black Sea ports, effectively bringing the empire into **World War I** on the side of the Central Powers. This move was controversial within Ottoman society. The CUP leadership believed that a successful war effort—especially against Russia—could allow the empire to reclaim lost territories and revitalize its standing as a major power.

Key Fronts

- **Caucasus Campaign**: Ottoman forces clashed with Russia in harsh winter conditions. Early disasters, such as **Sarıkamış (1914–1915)**, cost tens of thousands of Ottoman troops.
- **Gallipoli (1915–1916)**: A brighter spot for Ottoman morale, where the army under Mustafa Kemal repelled a massive Allied amphibious invasion, boosting the empire's confidence and prestige.
- **Mesopotamia and Palestine**: Long campaigns against British forces seeking to control the Tigris-Euphrates region and the Levant, culminating in eventual Ottoman defeats.

Domestic Turmoil

War demands overwhelmed an already strained economy, leading to rampant inflation and shortages. The government requisitioned supplies from rural communities, fueling resentment. Meanwhile, concerns over loyalty and suspicion of internal "fifth columns" influenced drastic policies, the most tragic being the **Armenian deportations and mass killings (1915)**—an event that devastated Armenian communities in eastern Anatolia and remains heavily contested in its historical interpretation.

CHAPTER 20

THE EMPIRE'S FINAL DECADES AND LEGACY

The **Ottoman Empire's** decision to enter **World War I** alongside Germany and Austria-Hungary in 1914 marked the beginning of its final chapter. Although the empire initially scored notable victories—such as at Gallipoli—it was ultimately overwhelmed by resource shortages, internal revolts, and the might of the Allied war machine. By the war's end in 1918, Ottoman state structures were on the verge of collapse, and Allied powers occupied key regions, determined to partition what remained of the empire. This final chapter explores the tumultuous period from the empire's wartime experiences to the postwar treaties that dismantled it, concluding with reflections on the Ottoman legacy that continues to influence regional identities, laws, and cultures to this day.

1. THE STRESSES OF WORLD WAR I ON THE OTTOMAN HOME FRONT

War Exhaustion and Economic Breakdown

From 1914 to 1918, the Ottoman state struggled to sustain multiple fronts. The **Committee of Union and Progress (CUP)** regime directed all resources toward the war effort, leading to critical shortages in civilian sectors. Key imports—like medical supplies, machinery, and foodstuffs—dwindled. Urban populations faced skyrocketing prices, while rural areas suffered requisitions of grain and livestock. Malnutrition and disease epidemics, including cholera and typhus, spread among both soldiers and civilians.

Social and Demographic Upheavals

The war also accelerated demographic shifts. Refugees from the Balkans and the Caucasus flooded Anatolia, requiring state assistance that was increasingly hard to provide. Simultaneously, the empire's Christian minorities—especially Armenians—experienced mass deportations, seizures of property, and large-scale mortality. Although the government justified these measures as a military necessity, critics and historians have widely condemned them, underscoring the scale of suffering and the long-term ramifications for Ottoman society.

2. MILITARY FRONTS AND MAJOR CAMPAIGNS

Gallipoli: A Symbol of Stubborn Defense

The **Gallipoli Campaign (1915–1916)** became a rare source of pride for the Ottomans during the war. Allied forces (Britain, France, and Anzac troops) attempted to seize the straits to knock the Ottomans out of the conflict. Under the leadership of commanders like **Mustafa Kemal (Atatürk)**, Ottoman defenders entrenched in rugged terrain, repelling repeated Allied assaults. Although immensely costly in lives, Gallipoli bolstered the empire's morale and temporarily thwarted Allied aims in the east.

Middle East Theater: Mesopotamia and Palestine

- **Mesopotamia**: British troops advanced from the Persian Gulf, capturing Basra and ultimately **Baghdad (1917)**. The Ottoman defense, hampered by poor infrastructure and desert conditions, crumbled.
- **Palestine**: British campaigns, led by General Allenby, pushed the Ottomans out of Jerusalem (1917) and ultimately took Damascus (1918) with assistance from Arab nationalist forces galvanized by the **Arab Revolt**—fomented by British agents like **T. E. Lawrence (Lawrence of Arabia)**.

The Caucasus Front

In the Caucasus, Ottoman forces endured harsh winters and mountainous battles. Russian advances into eastern Anatolia, combined with Kurdish tribal dynamics and local Armenian populations, shaped a volatile frontier. Although the Russian Revolution (1917) led to Russia's withdrawal from the war, the devastation already inflicted in the region deepened the empire's crises.

3. POLITICAL CRISIS AND THE ARMISTICE OF MUDROS (1918)

Dissolution of the CUP Triumvirate

As Allied gains mounted in 1918, the CUP's position collapsed. Leading figures like Enver Pasha, Talat Pasha, and Cemal Pasha fled into exile, recognizing that defeat was imminent. A caretaker government under Sultan **Mehmed VI** (r. 1918–1922) sought an armistice to spare Istanbul and avert total occupation.

The Armistice of Mudros

Signed on October 30, 1918, the **Armistice of Mudros** effectively ended Ottoman participation in World War I. Its terms granted the Allies the right to occupy strategic points within the empire and control key ports and railways. Ottoman demobilization began immediately, with large swaths of territory falling under Allied or local nationalist occupations. The centuries-long empire was, for all intents and purposes, reduced to an Istanbul-based administration struggling to assert any meaningful sovereignty.

4. THE POSTWAR TREATIES AND PARTITION SCHEMES

The Paris Peace Conference and Ottoman Question

In 1919, the victorious Allied powers convened in Paris to redraw the world map. The so-called **"Eastern Question"** loomed large, as Britain, France, Italy, and Greece each expected to carve out spheres of influence or direct territorial acquisitions in Ottoman lands. Nationalist Arab leaders, having fought alongside the Allies, demanded independent Arab states. Armenian representatives sought an Armenian homeland in eastern Anatolia. Amid these competing claims, the Ottoman delegation found itself marginalized.

The Treaty of Sèvres (1920)

The resulting **Treaty of Sèvres** envisioned dismantling Ottoman domains. Key provisions included:

1. **Stripping Thrace and much of the Aegean coast** for Greece.
2. **Placing eastern Anatolia** under an Armenian state mandate, though never fully implemented due to local resistance and shifting Allied priorities.
3. **Awarding spheres of influence** in Anatolia to France and Italy.
4. **Internationalizing the Straits**, removing Ottoman control over the Bosporus and Dardanelles.

Sultan Mehmed VI, reliant on Allied goodwill to preserve his throne, reluctantly acquiesced. But the treaty lacked legitimacy in the eyes of many Ottoman officers and nationalists, who considered it a direct assault on Turkish sovereignty.

5. THE RISE OF TURKISH NATIONALISM AND THE WAR OF INDEPENDENCE

Mustafa Kemal and the National Resistance

Rejecting the Treaty of Sèvres, Ottoman officers—most famously **Mustafa Kemal** (later Atatürk)—organized resistance in **Anatolia**. They convened national congresses in Erzurum and Sivas (1919), rallying local populations against foreign occupation and the perceived puppet regime in Istanbul. The movement established a **Grand National Assembly** in Ankara, effectively challenging the sultan's authority.

Conflict with Occupying Forces

Between 1920 and 1922, the nationalist forces clashed with Greek armies advancing into western Anatolia, while also negotiating with France, Italy, and Soviet Russia to secure diplomatic and military backing. Sultan Mehmed VI could do little as the nationalists built a parallel government, culminating in the defeat of Greek forces near the Sakarya River (1921) and the reconquest of the Aegean coast in 1922.

6. THE ABOLITION OF THE SULTANATE (1922)

Mehmed VI Deposed

As nationalist forces closed in on Istanbul, the last Ottoman sultan, **Mehmed VI**, found himself powerless. In November 1922, the **Grand National Assembly** abolished the Ottoman sultanate, ending the 600-year reign of the Osmanoğlu dynasty. Mehmed VI fled the capital aboard a British warship, marking the symbolic end of the empire. A brief caliphate—stripped of temporal power—lingered under **Abdülmecid II**, but that too would be abolished in 1924, under the new Turkish Republic.

Treaty of Lausanne (1923)

The subsequent **Treaty of Lausanne** recognized the sovereignty of the new Turkish state under nationalist leadership, nullifying the dismemberment plans of Sèvres. While this treaty established the Republic of Turkey's borders, it definitively confirmed the **Ottoman Empire's** demise. Other regions—such as the Arab provinces—had already fallen under French and British mandates, shaping the modern Middle East.

7. THE EMPIRE'S LEGACY IN SUCCESSOR STATES

Impact on the Middle East

The **Arab provinces** formed new political entities under European mandates: Syria and Lebanon under France; Iraq, Transjordan, and Palestine under Britain. Although these nations later gained independence, their borders, governance structures, and communal tensions often reflected the Ottoman administrative legacies and the abrupt partition orchestrated by the Allies.

Balkan States

The empire's withdrawal from the Balkans facilitated the rise of national states—Serbia, Bulgaria, Greece, Romania—each forging national narratives rooted in liberation from Ottoman rule. However, Ottoman influences persisted in architecture, law codes, cuisine, and demographics, reminding these societies of a shared though contested past.

Modern Turkey

In Anatolia, the core Ottoman lands formed the foundation of the **Republic of Turkey** in 1923. While the new republic's leaders disavowed many Ottoman institutions—secularizing the state, adopting the Latin alphabet, and abolishing the caliphate—they also inherited Ottoman legal precedents, a tradition of central administration, and a deep cultural syncretism that continued to shape Turkey's evolving identity.

8. CULTURAL AND SOCIAL INHERITANCE

Legal Systems and Administration

Many successor states adapted Ottoman legal frameworks, especially the **Tanzimat**-influenced civil and commercial codes. Even as they introduced nationalist or colonial legal reforms, the layering of Ottoman institutions persisted in forms of land tenure, tax collection, and local governance councils.

Architectural and Artistic Legacies

Mosques, bridges, caravanserais, and palaces built under centuries of Ottoman patronage remained vibrant landmarks in cities from the Balkans to North Africa. Ottoman influences in music, miniature painting, calligraphy, and folk traditions continued to resonate, though sometimes overshadowed by new nationalist aesthetics or European styles.

Linguistic and Culinary Traces

A distinctive culinary tradition, blending Central Asian, Middle Eastern, and Mediterranean flavors, took shape over centuries of Ottoman rule. Even after the empire's demise, dishes like börek, baklava, and coffee culture maintained popularity across multiple successor states. Linguistic cross-pollination also endured: Balkan languages incorporate Turkish loanwords, while Turkish itself absorbed Persian, Arabic, and local Balkan terms.

9. HISTORIOGRAPHY AND PERSPECTIVES ON OTTOMAN DECLINE

The Decline Narrative Debated

For generations, many Western and nationalist historians framed the empire's late history as a story of **inevitable decline** from a golden age under Süleiman the Magnificent. More recent scholarship questions this linear view, highlighting that the empire adapted in multiple waves—through Tanzimat reforms and constitutional experiments—and only collapsed under the extraordinary pressures of World War I and the ensuing global realignments.

Ottomanism, Pan-Islamism, and Other Ideologies

Throughout the 19th and early 20th centuries, ideologies such as **Ottomanism**, which sought to unify all subjects under a supra-ethnic imperial identity, and **Pan-Islamism**, emphasizing the sultan's caliphal role, competed with emergent nationalism. These varied responses to modernity complicate simplistic narratives of "decay," revealing a state continuously seeking renewal in the face of external and internal challenges.

10. CONCLUSION OF CHAPTER 20 (AND OF THIS HISTORY)

From its humble beginnings as a frontier beylik in the late 13th century to its sprawling heights under sultans like Mehmed II and Süleiman the Magnificent, the **Ottoman Empire** shaped the political, economic, and cultural destinies of lands spanning three continents. Over six centuries, it evolved from a warrior state grounded in frontier ghazi traditions to a multi-ethnic, multi-religious empire that graphed diverse peoples into an imperial mosaic. Repeatedly, it adapted to shifting circumstances—Mongol threats, European military revolutions, global trade realignments, and internal reform movements—yet the empire's final downfall came when the cataclysm of World War I laid bare its remaining vulnerabilities.

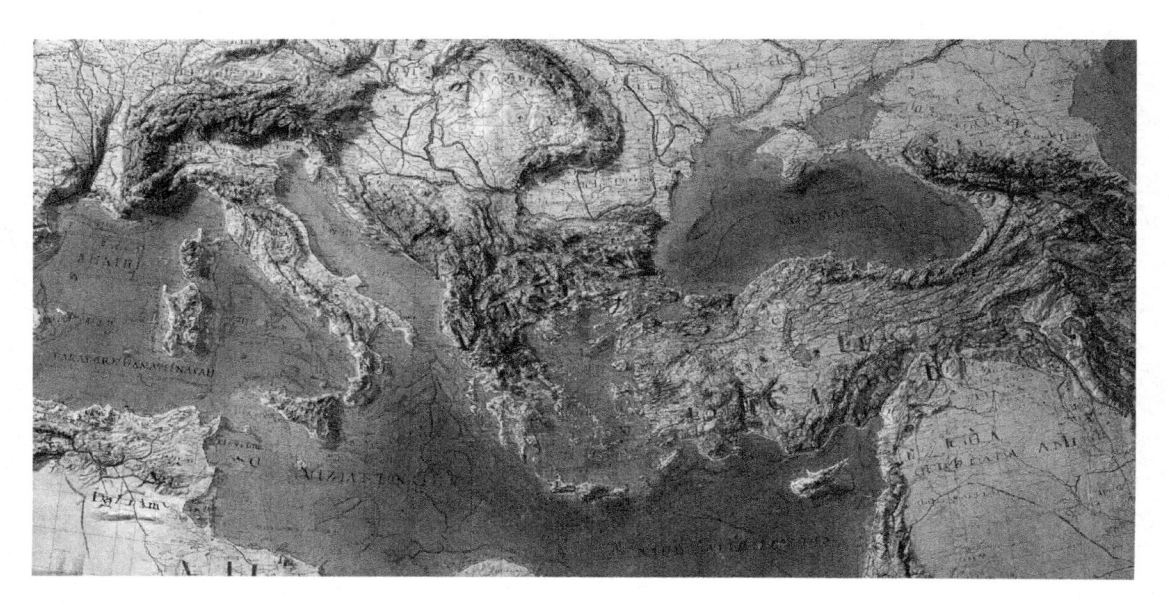

In its aftermath, new states rose from Ottoman domains: modern Turkey, the Balkan nations, and several Arab countries under European mandates. Nonetheless, the Ottoman legacy endures. Legal codes, urban landscapes, culinary practices, and shared cultural idioms continue to unite post-Ottoman societies. Historians still debate the empire's strengths and weaknesses, its achievements in governance and culture, and the lessons it offers about managing diversity within a centralized imperial framework.

While the Ottoman Empire no longer exists as a political entity, its **600-year** history remains a testament to human adaptability, resilience, and the entangled narratives of conquest, reform, and survival. Its story resonates today in the architecture of Istanbul, the multiethnic neighborhoods of the Balkans, the culinary traditions of the Middle East, and the ongoing discussions of how best to balance tradition with modernization. Thus concludes our exploration of **The Complete History of the Ottoman Empire**, an epic saga of one of the most influential states in world history.

Help Us Share Your Thoughts!

Dear reader,

Thank you for spending your time with this book. We hope it brought you enjoyment and a few new ideas to think about. If there was anything that didn't work for you, or if you have suggestions on how we can improve, please let us know at **kontakt@skriuwer.com**. Your feedback means a lot to us and helps us make our books even better.

If you enjoyed this book, we would be very grateful if you left a review on the site where you purchased it. Your review not only helps other readers find our books, but also encourages us to keep creating more stories and materials that you'll love.

By choosing Skriuwer, you're also supporting **Frisian**—a minority language mainly spoken in the northern Netherlands. Although **Frisian** has a rich history, the number of speakers is shrinking, and it's at risk of dying out. Your purchase helps fund resources to preserve and promote this language, such as educational programs and learning tools. If you'd like to learn more about Frisian or even start learning it yourself, please visit **www.learnfrisian.com**.

Thank you for being part of our community. We look forward to sharing more books with you in the future.

Warm regards,
The Skriuwer Team

Printed in Dunstable, United Kingdom